TRAINING
YOUR OWN
SERVICE DOG

Step By Step Guide To An Obedient Service Dog

Training Your Own Service Dog

Step by Step Guide to an Obedient Service Dog

Max Matthews

Table of Contents

Additionally, the information in the following pages is intended only for informational purposes and should thus be thought of as universal. As befitting its nature, it is presented without assurance regarding its prolonged validity or interim quality. Trademarks that are mentioned are done without written consent and can in no way be considered an endorsement from the trademark holder.

Introduction

Congratulations on your first step to training your very own service dog! This exciting journey you are about to embark (no pun intended) will seamlessly guide you through the basics and complexities of selecting and training a service dog. If you are dealing with emotional trauma or any physical disabilities, I'd like you to think of this book as a *bone*-a fide (okay, that pun was intended) self-help book. Not only does training your own dog create an inseparable bond between you and your canine, but it also lets you achieve small goals that can benefit you and your dog. Not to mention, it will give you an element of your life that you can control.

In this book, we will guide you all throughout the process – from choosing your service dog, teaching basic skills, producing reliable obedience, preparing for the ADI Public Access Test, to teaching your dog amazing, helpful tasks. Included in this book is a wide variety of tasks and skills your dog can learn for different types of disabilities.

I know you might be thinking, "How long is this going to take?" Well, the truth is, it's up to you and your dog! Your dog has the mental capacity of that of a three or four-year-old human child. Also, dogs are unique and they learn in different ways. That means, the time it would take for your dog to learn a certain task or skill depends on his maturity and capability to follow orders. Whether your dog is a fast-learner or not, you need to have patience. It's the very key to be successful in the whole training process. This book provides tips on how to troubleshoot your dog if he or she is having a difficulty following an order. This will help smoothen the progression of the training.

Additionally, this book will give you a deeper understanding of the etiquette and laws regarding service dogs, professional training terminology, and the mental and physical tools you'll need in order to be successful in this endeavor. I have laid the book out in stages of progression. It is important to not skip the steps in the process and to build a solid foundation on which you will shape your personalized service dog. Please enjoy!

Chapter 1: Service Dog Laws and Tests

First and foremost, any responsible service dog owner/handler should be well versed in the legalities respecting the service dog community. In this chapter, we will cover what is going to be expected from you, your companion, and the general public from here on out.

Under the Americans with Disabilities Act (ADA), a service dog is defined as, "A dog that has been individually trained to do work or perform tasks for an individual with a disability." Disabilities include but are not limited to; mobility issues, sensory issues, diabetes, multiple sclerosis, autism, epilepsy, and Post-Traumatic Stress Disorder (PTSD) to name a few. If your disability is not listed, you are still eligible to have a service dog if you are unable to perform a function considered normal/easy to most without the use of a service dog. Functions such as eating, remembering, seeing, hearing and standing are all examples.

As the ADA states, regardless of the laws of your apartment building or rental property, you are given the right to live with your service dog. This also exempts them from any pet deposit fee as they are seen an essential part of your quality of life and *not* a pet. The same applies to hotels, they cannot charge you a pet fee. The two places a service dog is not allowed (due to health codes) is an operating room in a hospital and a food preparation kitchen at a restaurant.

Later in this book, we will discuss how your dog should behave in public, but what about the people? When you go out in public, there are a few things to remember. First, not everyone will accept a dog in uncommon places such as restaurants, libraries, or hospitals. Second, no matter how upset they are here is what they can't do; ask you to leave, ask what your disability is, and ask for proof of your disability or service dog certification. You can deter some of these questions (that may be asked anyway) by attaching a vest labeled service dog and/or an ID on his/her vest or collar. However, a business owner or person is allowed to ask you what task your dog performs for you. As an example, if your dog acts as a barrier between you and people behind you (often for veterans who are given anxiety by being in line with someone standing too closely behind them) you may tell them the action your dog performs but do not have to explain why. Another example is if your service dog is trained to remind you to take medication at a certain time, you may explain the task but do not have to disclose the medication or what it is taken for.

Flying with your service dog is important, especially because one of the services your dog may provide you with is emotional support on a flight. Luckily, ADA law has given you the right to bring them on the plane with you right by your side without having to pay any fees regarding your dog. Please remember, only one service dog is allowed on any given flight at a time. You will also be boarded first just as anyone with a wheelchair is. Below I have provided you with a few airlines and their guidelines.

Alaska Air:

- No charge

- Visible indication such as a vest or collar preferred

- Verbal assurance of your service dog's task required if an inquiry is made by airline personnel

- Service dogs who are properly harnessed may sit at the individual's feet, except if they are too large obstructing the aisle or area used for emergency exits.

American Airlines:

- No charge

- Visible indication such as a vest or collar preferred

- Verbal assurance of your service dog's task required if an inquiry is made by airline personnel

Jet Blue:

- Visible indication such as a vest or collar required

- Verbal assurance of your service dog's task required if an inquiry is made by airline personnel

- Documentation is also accepted

US Airlines:

- One of the following is required; animal ID card, harness or tags, written documentation, credible verbal assurance

Virgin Airlines:

- One of the following is required; animal ID card, harness of tags, or credible verbal assurance.

Although you do not need to be a professional in order to train your dog, you do need to take a Public Access Test. This is a test created to ensure the validity of the basic training put into a service dog. This does not include tasks trained to aid your disability. In order to take the test, a minimum of 120 hours of training should be invested into your dog beforehand. This should take about six months. In the test, no treats or leash corrections are allowed. Throughout the book, we will set up for the goal of eliminating these two factors, so you aren't dependent on them. The dog should not show any aggression or fear, and if s/he does, s/he will be disqualified.

The Assistant Dog International (ADI) Public Access Test: Here is a general outline of what this test consists of. The evaluator and you will agree on location suitable for the test. S/he will be responsible for bringing an assistant person, plate of food, assistant dog, and access to a shopping cart.

- **Control Unloading Your Dog from a Vehicle:** First unload any necessary equipment such as wheelchair, crutches, canes, etc. Once this is done, the dog may be released from the vehicle and wait for further instruction from the handler. The dog must not run around off leash or ignore any commands given by the handler. Once the handler and dog are settled, an assistant with a dog will walk by about six feet away from you. Both dogs must remain calm and under control. They should not be trying to get to one another.

- **Approaching the Establishment:** After the first exercise is completed, you and your dog will navigate through the parking lot towards the building of the agreed upon location. Your dog must stay in a relative heel position next to you and may not be allowed to forge ahead or lag behind. When cars or other distractions present themselves, your dog must not show fear towards them. If you stop for any reason, your dog must do so also.

- **Controlled Entry Through Doorway:** Walking through the threshold of the building, you must remain in control and pass safely through the doorway. Once inside, your dog may not be allowed to abandon the relative heel position and must not solicit any attention from anyone.

- **Heeling Through the Building:** You must demonstrate control of your dog as you walk through the building. Your dog should not be more than a foot away from you and must be able to walk through crowds of people keeping up with your pace. S/he must slow down to meet your pace and stop promptly when you do. Turning corners should be prompt, and they should not lag. If in a tight space, your dog should be able to navigate safely through without damaging any merchandise around him/her. The only exception to tension on the lead is if s/he is pulling your wheelchair.

- **Six Foot Recall on Lead:** Once in an open area, you will be prompted by your evaluator to perform a six-foot recall. On a six foot (or longer) leash, you will leave your dog in a stay, turn and call your dog to you. This must be an effortless and quick action. The dog must not dredge or solicit attention from strangers. Upon return, your dog must come close enough to be readily touched.

- **Sit on Command:** There will be three individual times you will be asked to sit your dog. Each time, the dog should respond quickly with no more than two repetitions of the command. The first sit will be situated next to a plate of food. You are allowed to verbally or physically correct your dog for sniffing the food but once this has been done your dog should remain sitting and ignore the food completely. S/he will not be taunted by the food. For the second sit, you will be asked to sit your dog and then the evaluator's assistant will walk passed you within three feet away with a shopping cart. Your dog must not show any fear towards the cart. If s/he starts to move you are allowed to correct him/her in order to maintain the sit. Finally, your dog must maintain a sit while the evaluator's assistant walks up behind you and your dog, then begins a conversation with you and pets your dog. Your dog must not break his/her position to solicit attention from the assistant. You may be allowed to verbally repeat yourself to encourage the stay or give a physical correction.

- **Down on Command:** Similar to exercise six, down on command will include multiple exercises with a few variations. For the first down, you will be seated at a table with your dog in a down underneath the table out of the way. Food will then be dropped off of the table, and your dog must maintain his/her position and not break to eat or sniff the food. You will be allowed to give verbal or physical corrections. Once the second down is executed, an adult and child will approach you and your dog, s/he shall not break his/her position and not solicit attention. The child may pet your dog, and your dog should again maintain his/her stay.

- **Noise Distraction:** Whilst you and your dog are heeling through the building, the evaluator will drop his/her clipboard behind you. Your dog may jump and/or turn but must quickly recover and return to heeling along with you. Any excessive fear or aggression exhibited as a result of being started will conclude the test, and you will be disqualified.

- **Restaurant:** Like exercise seven (in fact this is most likely the time number seven will be tested), your dog will be in a down under your table. While being seated, your dog should refrain from showing interest in other tables and people as you walk by. Once seated s/he should not be obstructing the aisle in any way. Your dog will be allowed to move slightly (stand spin and lay down) in order to be comfortable as long as they don't require a lot of correcting or reminding.

- **Off Lead:** while heeling through the building, at some point your evaluator will prompt you to drop your leash. You will continue walking as your dog acknowledges the leash has been dropped. Although it will vary greatly depending on your disability, the test's purpose is to demonstrate you can remain in control of your dog and regain the leash.

- **Separation:** The evaluator's assistant will take your dog's leash from you and passively hold the dog without giving him/her any commands while you walk 20 feet away. Your dog must remain calm, collected and not show any sign of excessive stress, whining or barking. Any aggression will result in disqualification as well.

- **Controlled Exit:** Similar to the way you entered the building, you and your dog must safely leave through the threshold in a controlled manner and navigate back through the parking lot. S/he must not show any signs of aggression or fear when faced with traffic noises, cars or other distractions.

- **Controlled Loading into the Vehicle:** Once at the vehicle, your dog must wait patiently and not wander while you load your equipment into the car. Then safely load your dog.

- **Team Relationship:** Throughout the test, you and your dog should both be in a calm state and work well together with little to no adversity. Both of you should promote positivity to the public and maintain a relaxed demeanor.

It would also behoove you to participate in the Canine Good Citizen Test. This is a great way to document that you've put the training into your dog to ensure they are safe to take out in public with children, other people, and dogs. This test should be done without his/her service vest on. (More on that later in the book)

Canine Good Citizen Test: Some of these exercises you will recognize from the Public Access Test.

- **Friendly Stranger:** Your dog must sit by your side patiently while a stranger/evaluator approaches you. The evaluator will then usually shake your hand and have a normal short conversation with you. Your pup should show zero fear, aggression, or shyness and remain neutral to the presence of the stranger who will be ignoring him/her.

- **Sitting Politely for Petting:** Your dog must not show any disdain or shyness towards the evaluator while s/he pets his/her head and body. You may reassure your dog while this test is taking place.

- **Appearance and Grooming:** It is important that your dog is physically pleasing to the eye and clean for places like hospitals and restaurants. This test not only demonstrates your dog's neutrality to being groomed but also assess his/her health (including proper weight and mentally alert). The evaluator will inspect his/her ears, paws, and gums. Then, softly and naturally comb your dog's fur.

- **Walking on a Loose Leash**: Often given a pre-planned course of direction, you will be expected to walk your dog on a loose leash. It should be clear that your dog's attention is on you and where you're walking. This is to demonstrate your control over your dog when walking and changing direction. There should be at least one right turn, left turn and halt.

- **Walking Through a Crowd:** According to the American Kennel Club, a crowd of people consists of at least three people. You and your dog must politely walk through the crowd of the people without putting any strain on the leash.

- **Sit, Down, and Stay on Command:** Before the test, your dog's leash is replaced with a 20-foot leash. You will sit your dog, then tell them to down. Once your dog is in his/her down position, you will leave your dog. You may say stay, or if you have built the stay into your dog's down, you can simply leave your dog's side. At a natural pace, you will leave your dog's side walking forward and then turn at the end of the leash and return to your dog calmly. S/he must remain in the position you left them in until the evaluator gives further instruction.

- **Recall:** Similar to the stay exercise, you will leave your dog and walk 10 feet away. Once you are 10 feet away, you will turn and face your dog and call him/her.

- **Reaction to Another Dog:** This test's purpose is to demonstrate how your dog behaves around other dogs. From 20 feet away, you and another handler accompanied by their dog will begin walking towards each other. Your dog must not show any exuberance, fear, or aggression towards the approaching dog. Once you reach each other, you will stop, shake hands and exchange small talk. The dogs may acknowledge each other's presence but may not be overly interested. Then, you will continue walking past each other another 10 feet. Your dog must continue with you and not focus on the dog behind them.

- **Reaction to distraction:** During this test, the evaluator will present you and your dog with two distractions. Your dog must remain confident during this time. S/he should not bark, or panic by showing fear or aggression. Some examples of distractions you may be exposed to during the test are an opening umbrella, a jogger running by, a chair dropping, or dropping a crutch or cane.

- **Supervised Separation:** The goal of this test is to demonstrate that your dog can be left with a trusted friend or family member while you leave and go out of sight from your dog. During this exercise, your dog must remain under control of whoever has the leash. The evaluator takes the leash from you, and you leave out of sight for up to three minutes. S/he must not whine, bark, or pace during this time.

The only collars allowed during the Canine Good Citizen Test are flat collars and choke collars made of nylon, leather, or chain. Prong collars, halters, and electric collars are not allowed. You may also use a body harness or vest for your dog. Your evaluator will supply the long line. However, you are responsible for bringing your own brush or comb.

Reward items such as toys and food are not allowed during the test. You may, however, pet your dog in between exercises. With an exception of the last exercise being outside, your dog must not eliminate during the test. If s/he does, they will be disqualified. Any aggression exhibited by your dog will also result in disqualification.

It is imperative that your service dog is kept healthy and clean. Being a member of society means s/he must smell at least neutral and look clean. A service dog's nails are to be remolded and short to avoid damaging any objects s/he may come across in public such as store shelves. It is wise to carry a brush, comb, and sanitary wipes with you every day. Shedding must be kept to a minimum, many restaurants are reluctant to serve service dogs because of the owners who do not keep their shedding under control, and other reasons. The sanitary wipes are more so for the health of your dog. The world is a disgusting place, and the ground is covered in germs. It is important to check your dog's paw pads regularly to make sure they are clean and safe. For instance, if you were at the mechanics, walking on the garage floor or even a parking lot your dog could potentially pick up oils from cars on his/her pads and then subsequently ingest the oils from licking their paws.

Chapter 2: Selection

Just as I stated in the introduction, each dog is unique in a way that its trainability may vary from Forest Gump to Albert Einstein. The good news is you can improve on this through training. However, there are some traits a dog could possess which are not easy to manipulate. This is why it is important to remember that genetics play a crucial role in the training process and overall outcome of your service dog. Think back to the bulk of service dogs you've seen, what breeds come to mind? Most likely you're thinking of Labradors, Golden Retrievers, and Poodle mixes. There's a reason! A large fraction of the professionally trained service dogs has been specifically bred for this work. These traits include handler dependency, mild energy level, solid nerves, and overall health. Even when carefully bred and tested for these traits, a lot of the puppies born into this line of work are washed out and sent to pet homes.

This being said, if you do choose to go to a breeder to select your service dog candidate, please do not make your final decision based on the phrase, "Aw, he likes me!" Many people make the mistake of assuming if the dog "chooses you" that it's a perfect match. However, regardless of age, when it comes to selecting your superhero (*I mean service dog)*, your criteria must be based on what your disability demands of him or her.

In accordance to the ADA definition of a service dog, it is imperative that you keep in mind what will be expected from your dog. For instance, if you lack mobility, you would select a dog that already enjoys holding objects in his/her mouth. This will be beneficial to you down the road when you teach commands such as *bring, open/close,* and *hold.* For some dogs, holding objects in their mouth is unpleasant, whereas for other dogs, it is a delight to do so. Furthermore, a non-discriminate mouth (a trait a dog possesses that allows them to not care what they hold in their mouth) will lessen the chances of you becoming frustrated with your dog's unwillingness to do a task. Thus, hindering your training and potentially dampening your relationship.

Another example of mindful selection is focusing on inherit dependency (a trait a dog possesses that makes them focus more on their handler). This is a dog who is more comfortable sticking by his/her handler's side than s/he is exploring and finding value in something or someone else. After all, what good is a service dog that can't or won't focus on his/her job? Imagine your disability is Post-Traumatic Stress Disorder. Like many suffering with this, you become panicked and stressed when faced with large crowds. If you have a dog who is more so interested in what the crowd is doing, how is s/he supposed to calm your storms? A dog who is naturally dependent on his/her handler will look to them for the answer as a default behavior (a behavior a dog goes to when in doubt of what s/he should do) in situations like this. This trait will allow for a strong foundation since you will have to put forth less effort to be the prevailing focus for your dog in any given situation. A good way to test these factors is by playing fetch with the dog. If s/he bring the toy back to you by default it is safe to predict that the dog will be willing to work with humans and should make some of the tasks less frustrating to teach. A dog that doesn't bring it back and prefers to keep the toy to him/herself is showing signs that s/he may not be cooperative during task training and be more independent. Remember that anyone, including dogs, can have a bad day. Try these tests a few times over the course of a few weeks. Yes, of course any dog can be trained to retrieve objects but with this test you are assessing his/her eagerness to work with humans. Choosing a dog that does not naturally want to bring items back to you may need to be trained to do so with compulsion. This, although effective, requires more time and patience, and the dog will not enjoy his work as much as if s/he was willing. When testing, there are ways you can bring out this eagerness to retrieve if the dog you are testing is willing to please. These include using a clicker and reward for coming back with the toy or using another dog that does enjoy retrieving to elicit a competitive edge.

Earlier, we touched on common breeds used in this line of work. Labradors make wonderful service dogs as long as you get the right kind of Labrador. Dogs of the same breed are as similar as people of the same race. Yes, they have similar traits and physical features, but depending on their family tree they can differ greatly. Take for example a Field Lab – bred as a bird dog, extremely high energy. They're the labs that tear up your home and knock Grandma over (with love) as she walks through the door. On the other hand, you have the English Lab. Often more plump and happy with being a couch potato. Pop quiz: which one would you feel more comfortable with out in public? If you said the Field Lab, you're insane and should re-read Chapter One. Now, that's not to say you can't choose a dog that is low energy and also enjoys long walks or even hikes. However, an even-keeled service dog is much more likely to be content resting when his/her job calls for accompanying you to dinner at a fancy restaurant, reading in the library, or taking notes in a classroom or lecture hall.

This mellow attitude often plays a role in the dog's nerves. We've all seen it, the family dog is sleeping on the floor, and someone accidentally steps on his/her tail. The dog both jumps up and runs away, acts out in aggression, or they're barely fazed by it. The two actions come down to fight or flight (an inherent defense all animals possess that is triggered by perceived danger. Either the animal responds by running away or aggressing towards the danger) but the third is ideal. When a dog has good nerves, this means s/he is capable of maintaining composure in seemingly stressful situations. This doesn't mean if a dog jumps in the air when a metal dog bowl hits the concrete floor that the dog is garbage. As long as the dog recovers, this can be worked on. How quickly a dog recovers from being startled will tell you how easy or difficult it will be to desensitize him/her to noises and new environments. When you select a dog with a long recovery time, you will most likely be spending most of your training getting your dog comfortable in a new environment. This takes away from working on their obedience and tasks in public. If you try to work on these things while they are in a nervous state, you will not only make little to no progress, but you will also create a negative association with those commands and tasks. You can test for recovery time by randomly dropping an object such as a metal bowl, book, chip bag, or anything that may cause a startled reaction. If the dog darts away and cowers, s/he will most likely not be a good candidate for service work. If s/he startles and ducks but resumes his/her natural posture, this is a good indication that s/he will take less energy to adapt to new environments and stressful situations. S/he will do well once the desensitization training starts. Bonus points to the dog that doesn't flinch and investigates the fallen object!

There will be times where other people will accidentally step on your dog's tail. This will mostly happen when your dog is laying by you while you are eating or other situations where you are sitting in public. Take it as a compliment! It is imperative that your dog be desensitized to touch because accidents happen and a dog that is not accustomed to this stimulus will create a scene defeating the purpose of having a service dog; to improve your quality of life. To test for this, start by simply petting the dog. A dog that is easily excited by touch is a poor choice. Lightly hold the dog's ears, muzzle and then jowls. It is okay if the dog is curious as to what you are doing. However, s/he should not react aggressively (mouthing is not aggression and should be expected as dogs explore with their mouths). Next, move to the paws. Run your hands down the dog's legs and grasp his/her feet. Apply even pressure to the dog's paw and then gently pinch the webbing in between his/her toes. Note the dog's reaction. The more accepting s/he is of your invasiveness, the more likely they will shape up to be a reliable and level-headed companion in situations such as getting stepped on, vet visits, and the occasional obnoxious, or unpermitted child in your dog's face. If the dog is unforgiving towards the tester, this may not be the best choice as s/he may hold grudges that could get in the way of training.

Being that your end goal is to successfully complete the ADA Public Access Test, it would behoove you to test your candidates with this in mind. This means that your candidates should easily be able to get in and out of vehicles for which you would need to assess the dog's physical health for this action, and his/her willingness to jump into and out of a vehicle. While we are on the subject of cars, your service dog will need to be able to compose him/herself next to moving cars and busy traffic. It is okay if your prospective dog is a little cautious, but resorting to a fight or flight response is not a good sign. If you are able to bring your candidate into a store that allows dogs, observe the way they navigate isles and maneuver around displays and in tight spaces. The dog should display confidence and not be overly interested in other people, especially not trying to solicit attention from the public. The energy level of a dog is important to observe in this environment. S/he should not be overly excited to see people/children, or dogs, and should not tamper with any displays or merchandise. Alternatively, a dog that slinks through the aisles and is reluctant to pass through thresholds would most likely wind up needing more rehabilitation than routine training.

Many times, good service dog candidates can be found in rescues and shelters. Don't worry, if you'd like to change his/her name take solace in the fact that dogs are very adaptive and, when done properly, your dog will snap his/her head around and the sound of their new name. Some dogs even respond to nicknames to associate to the actions of the human. If you choose to buy from a breeder, it is important to ask to know about the temperament and energy level of the dogs they have bred. Pure breeds I would suggest are labs, golden retrievers, and flat-coated retrievers. Ultimately, it is up to you what breed you would like. If you choose a breed that generally holds a stigma of being "mean," be aware that you may run into the occasional person who will voice their ignorant opinion on this. Ask yourself, "Do I want to defend my dog every time I go out?" I have seen this with Military Veterans where they train up their Pitbull to be their service dog, and even though the dog behaves perfectly, the public presents an issue with the dog's presence. This will inevitably add stress to your life instead of improving its quality. People who have experienced this pitfall end up spending more time at home instead of going out in public. This does not only dampens your quality of life but will also cause your dog's obedience to slack off. Maintenance is important to keeping their obedience sharp. If you or someone you live with has allergies, I recommend seeking out a breeder of Australian Labradoodles. There is a big difference between Golden Doodles, Labradoodles, and Australian Labradoodles. Most of the Golden Doodles and Labradoodles that you see have got their genetic makeup more so from the higher energy lineages of bird dogs. Poodles are also usually very hyperactive dogs. Mix these two together, and you get immature overly stimulated balls of ADHD. Not only are they antsy, but they are also often slow to mature making them have a puppy-like mentality far into adulthood. Moreover, you know puppies are often distra – SQUIRREL! This is fun for a pet home, not for a library. Alternatively, the Australian Labradoodle is specifically bred for service dog work. Not only are they hypo-allergenic, but they are also intelligent, even-tempered, and mature at a very quick rate. Often times they mature before the age of one.

Once you have selected the dog you believe will be the best fit, it is wise to have a probationary period where the dog lives with you for a month to confirm it is a good fit for you, your family, and your lifestyle. During this time, have the dog with you as much as possible, if you are prone to seizures or panic attacks ensure the dog is not fearful of these episodes. Not only is it important to observe his/her behavior during but also right before the seizure or panic attack happens. Some actions the dog may naturally exhibit are barking or whining, pawing, or jumping up on you. Spending extensive buddy time is very important. You see, when you spend a lot of time with a very close friend, you would immediately notice subtle changes in his behavior or mood. You would quickly notice when he's feeling bad or if something's bothering him. The same goes with dogs. The closer you are with your dog, the more they are able to know your feelings – if you feel uncomfortable, if you're sick, or if you are about to have a panic attack.

Since dogs rely on the order of events to decide what is worth remembering and responding to and what needs to be thrown out, they are masters at reading your poker face and picking up on those minuscule behaviors you exhibit before you succumb to a panic attack. Having them around you as much as possible will give you a better chance of seeing what his/her alert is and giving your dog more information to collect to be able to tell when the change happens. While it is a controversial topic whether dogs can detect seizures before they happen, they are able to recognize them as they are happening and can be trained to find help, retrieve a phone, or even stay with the person through the seizure. The ability of your dog to stay unflustered while getting you help in these situations is very important. That's why, while the dog is still on probation, you must ensure that the dog does not exhibit any sign of fear towards these episodes. It would take more time and energy to desensitize him/her to the situation and then ask them to perform a task while being stressed and afraid. It isn't fair to the dog. And *again*, it takes away the purpose of having a service dog.

Types of Services Dogs and What They Provide:

Allergen Alert Dogs: As humans, we have about 5 million olfactory receptors that help us conclude that a cake is being baked in the oven. However, dogs have 220 million receptors in their olfactory system that allow them to determine that there is a carrot cake being baked in the oven made with two cups all-purpose flour, two cups of sugar , one teaspoon salt, four eggs, three cups of carrot – I think you get the point. Their nose is so powerful they can pinpoint residual odor from where someone touched a doorknob and then take you right to that exact person. It is with this highly developed talent that they are able to alert sufferers of severe allergies to dangers in the area or even in their food.

For instance, say you are allergic to eggs. Your dog would be able to sniff the carrot cake previously mentioned and alert you that there are eggs baked into the contents of the cake. This is done by isolating the ingredient and creating a positive association with the scent and rewarding the dog for alerting to it. This can take more than a month to train to complete accuracy. This (like with other detection trained service dogs) taps into their natural instinct to hunt for scents and turns their life into a fun game where they are rewarded for finding a certain scent or scents.

Dogs are happiest when they are able to successfully use their natural instincts and be rewarded for it. A dog that is being selected for this line of work should be eager and able to focus on a scent to hunt. Independence and intelligence are also required if the dog is expected to constantly be on the lookout (or smellout – haha) for the allergen or allergens. The ideal handler is someone over the age of fifteen. This is because working a detection dog is not easy and there are a lot of idiosyncrasies that someone younger may miss. Please keep this in mind for other scent detection dogs listed in this book. One important thing to note about allergen detection dogs is that in order to maintain their training you must train them with the allergens you would normally not go near. You can take precautions like wearing latex gloves and keep the allergen in a vile with a small mesh top to limit contact. An allergen detection dog does not alert to the precursors of anaphylaxis. Many factors are to be taken into consideration with all detection dogs including the age of the odor, air flow, and physical barriers such as wrappers or sealed bags. The accuracy of your allergen dog will be predicated on these factors along with how often you maintain your training and your ability to work your dog. Most of the training application is done in a restaurant or in other public areas. This requires the dog to be able to work with distractions and competing scents. That being said, if you are allergic to more than one food or material, an allergen detection dog can successfully such for both simultaneously, and if one of them is present, they will alert you of the danger. It is not suggested that you train your own allergen alert dog as this is a work that needs to be very consistent and you may miss some of the idiosyncrasies during the training.

Diabetic Alert Dog: Many diabetics can feel the symptoms of their blood sugar dropping. However, some people who have had the disorder type 1 diabetes for a long time can develop a condition that is called Hypoglycemia Unawareness. Having this condition prevents you from being able to notice when you develop symptoms of low blood sugar including dizziness, shaking, and sweating. Without the knowledge of these symptoms to tell you to eat something in order to raise your blood glucose back to a regular level you can black out, have a seizure, or it could even result in a coma. Diabetics live in constant fear that this may happen at an unexpected time. To mitigate this fear and lessen the chance of having a seizure or blacking out, dogs are trained as detection dogs that alert to low glucose levels. The dogs are able to detect the low levels of glucose through the sweat secreted by their owners when they are experiencing hypoglycemia. To train these dogs, samples of sweat are collected by diabetes research facilities. These sweat samples are taken from patients who were experiencing either hyperglycemia (high blood glucose) or hypoglycemia (low blood glucose). Another way for diabetes alert dogs to detect the change in blood glucose levels is through their owner's breath. During hypoglycemia, your body exhales a chemical called isoprene, and it can be detected by a dog's nose. This is a less practiced way training. There are a number of ways your diabetes alert dog can respond to your changes in odor. Some of these include; dialing 911 on a special K9 phone, nudging your arm, jumping on your lap, licking you excessively, pawing at you, and/or retrieving your needed meditations to name a few.

Due to the severity of the importance of accuracy a Diabetes Alert Dog must have, it is not advised that you train your own. Not for the task of detection at least. Many months go into assuring the accuracy of these dogs. Due to the time consuming and tedious training put in, the training is very expensive. But take note, not all diabetics require a detection dog. Typically, only type one diabetics experience the issues associated with hypoglycemia. There are many factors that you can review to decide if a diabetes alert dog is right for you. For instance, if you don't have hypoglycemia unawareness but your blood glucose levels frequently fluctuate either dangerously high or dangerously low at night while you are asleep, a diabetes alert dog would be able to help you by waking you up when the change in levels is detected. Overall, if you are debilitated by the paranoia of hypoglycemia or hyperglycemia getting a diabetes alert dog could give you a better quality of life, lower your stress and anxiety attributed to your diabetes and promote a healthier lifestyle for you and allow you to take part in more physical activities. On top of the expenses associated with the training and purchasing of a diabetes alert dog, the waiting list can be anywhere between two to six months before a dog becomes available for you.

Post-Traumatic Stress Disorder Service Dogs: The first causes of Post-Traumatic Stress Disorder that usually comes to mind when you hear it is warfare combat. This disorder can be caused by any number of traumatic events that have happened in a person's life. For instance, I trained service dogs that were going to be matched up with young children who were rescued from sex trafficking. They often had nightmares, social anxiety, panic attacks as well as being untrusting and afraid around men and many more symptoms attributed to Post Traumatic Stress Disorder. Even a single event can leave a lasting scar in some people's lives such as a burglary, car crash, house fire, or assault. Many people get symptoms of this disorder after a traumatic event, but if the symptoms last more than six months, the individual is diagnosed with Post Traumatic Stress Disorder and may require a service dog to become more independent.

If you suffer from this disorder, reflect on how a dog could mitigate your life. Many sufferers need a dog that can interrupt panic attacks, remind them to take medication, create a barrier in public if they feel crowded, and aid your hyper-vigilance by clearing dark rooms and turning on lights. I have found that many people who suffer from Post-Traumatic Stress Disorder usually feel as though they are not in control in life and often times have feelings of hopelessness. What is so wonderful about the training involved especially when you are able to train your own dog from the ground up (even with professional help) it gives you a sense of control, and you are able to customize your training day to day. Many people I have worked with transform almost immediately once training starts. This is because they are setting small goals and achieving them. In other words, the training itself is therapeutic. Not only is the training rewarding, having a dog, in general, will force you to get out of bed in the morning because s/he needs to be taken care of. Giving the person a responsibility can push them to also take care of themselves. These dogs can even be trained to pull the blanket off of you in the morning to start the day.

As mentioned, children can be the handler of these dogs because the handling does not require any in-depth skill. Many children who suffer from this disorder can develop severe separation anxiety. Having a furry best friend by their side at all times can prove to be the best choice for giving them independence. Especially if they take pride in the training of their new companion.

Seeing Eye Dogs: Perhaps one of the most commonly thought of when service dogs are brought up, Seeing Eye Dogs or Guide Dogs act as the eyes of an individual who could otherwise not get around on his/her own due to loss of sight. For most people, walking around (especially in public) is easily taken for granted. However, for the visually impaired, it is difficult and dangerous. A Seeing Eye dog can mitigate dangers and difficulties by guiding the person to and from point A to point B while maneuvering around obstacles.

For instance, if you were walking down the street with your guide dog and needed to cross the road, your dog would be trained to stop at the curb every single time to let you know a curb was present. After this, you can safely cross the street without injury. Unless there is a car coming. If you were to try to continue into the street while a car was coming, your dog would firmly plant his/her feet to communicate to you that it is unsafe to walk. This is called *Intelligent Disobedience*. Dogs selected for this type of work must have a very high IQ. Intelligent disobedience is defined as an action a dog takes that is the opposite of what the handler is asking of them because they are aware that in given situation it is either unsafe or not applicable. Another example of this is when police K9s are searching a house for narcotics, and the handler attempts to guide the dog's search, but the dog decides to follow his/her highly developed nose instead of the guidance of his/her handler. In this case, s/he understands that in order to get rewarded you must follow the scent to source at all costs, even if it means being disobedient to the handler.

Due to the many hours and great amounts of hard work that must be put into these dogs, they are expensive. It is not recommended that the individual train his/her own Seeing Eye dog for public use because of the possible dangers you could face. However, in your own home, your dog can do a lot for you to mitigate your disability. Such tasks include retrieving items (often lost or misplaced), guiding you from room to room, helping you up if you have fallen, dialing 911 on their special service dog phone, reminding you to take medication and much more. Even so, it is suggested that you seek help for both the obedience and beginning stages of the task portion of your training as some of these can be complicated.

Hearing Assistance Dog: What's that? You have trouble hearing? A Hearing Assistance Dog could greatly improve your quality of life and safety. Many people who are deaf or hard of hearing have these service dogs in order to alert them to danger or even day to day noises. For instance, a new mother who is deaf may need to be alerted when her baby is crying. The dog will alert his/her owner by nudging their arm or pawing at them and then lead them to the noise, in this case, a crying baby. Other instances include but are not limited to alarms, phones ringing, someone calling their name, a moving car behind them, doorbells, etc. It is possible to train your own hearing assistance dog. Typically, Labradors and Golden Retrievers are the first choice when it comes to hearing assistance dogs, but other breeds can also do the work. Other popular dogs for this line of work include cocker spaniels, miniature poodles, and even Chihuahuas. This is often based on their temperament and personalities. Terrier mixes are also top picks and can be found at rescues and shelters.

As stated by Assistance Dog International; a hearing assistance dog must be trained on at least three or more different sounds. Like other requirements, they also insist the dog respond to his/her obedience promptly and behave professionally in public. Identification is required in the form of an identification card and harness or other type of equipment (such as a leash) that is clearly labeled showing that your dog is a service dog.

As mentioned, a hearing assistance dog can alert his/her owner of sounds and be trained to do this. However, even if not trained to alert to certain sounds in public, an alert dog is still extremely beneficial to his/her handler's disability. The handler can be more aware of their environment in general by watching their dog and his/her reactions to what is going on around them. For instance, if you are sitting on a bench and someone is walking up from behind you, you can watch your dog, and s/he will become alert to this cueing you to pay attention to what is behind you. This can be utilized best by teaching your dog which way to face when you are sitting down or even giving your dog a command to watch your back.

During your selection process, you should assess which dog is going to be most aware of his/her surrounding. A dog such as a Bassett hound may not be as vigilant as a terrier mix would be. Aside from being on the lookout, your dog must have a loving but independent temperament. A dog who is too dependent on his handler may not be focused on what is going on around him/her.

Mobility Assistance Dogs: There are a wide variety of mobility-related disabilities that require a service dog. People with muscular dystrophy, brain injuries, spinal cord injuries, ambulatory issues, amputations, or even arthritis are all candidate for a service dog, to name a few. People who have to live with balance related issues may use a dog who can help them stabilize and even remain stationary to help you up when you fall. If you do fall and cannot get up, these dogs can also be trained to seek help from someone in the house or dial 911 on their own special service dog phone. Those bound to a wheelchair may have difficulty getting up wheelchair ramps (depending on their physical condition). In this case, your dog would be trained to pull your wheelchair up the ramp. If you struggle with debilitating arthritis, you may need help undressing. Later in the book, we will teach your dog how to take off your jacket and socks. These techniques can be applied to more clothing if you need it to.

When selecting a mobility assistant dog, it is important to consider the tasks you will be training them to do. Aside from the obvious – mild tempered, intelligent dog – your dog should be able to support your weight if you need it to. The health of these dogs must also be assessed. Joint health is extremely important. If you have a wheelchair, they must be strong enough to pull it in a ramp if you should ever need them to. Breeds used for this type of work are usually livestock guardian dogs or mastiffs. These breeds include Great Pyrenees, Saint Bernard, Anatolian Shepherd, Bull Mastiff, etc.

These dogs are often equipped with special dog backpacks or handled harnesses so that their owners can have the dog carry items for them and also use them as a brace for balance and support. A mobility service dog can greatly improve the life of someone who would otherwise dread going into public. Without a service dog, this ordeal may be physically tiring, emotionally painful (wondering how they look in the public eye) and altogether not worth the energy. Once they get the service dog, not only are they more focused on the dog and his/her training needs (they need to go in public to maintain their training) the owner often feels that their public appearance has been changed in a positive way. Some people with mobility issues are unable to do things like shop by themselves because they can't reach certain items and it can be exhausting. In this book, we will go over some tasks you can teach your dog that will benefit you when you go to the grocery store.

Seizure Alert Dog: The topic of seizure Alert dogs is a controversial one in the service dog community. The idea is that a dog can be trained to detect a seizure before it happens. Although there are cases where dogs have done this successfully, it is not apparent how dogs are able to do this. Some speculate that they can hear the accelerated heart rate or that our skin secretes different chemicals prior to the seizure. Unfortunately, because we do not know how they are able to detect seizures, there is no guaranteed way to train for the behavior. My best suggestion is to spend as much time as possible with your dog, and over time they will notice slight changes in your behavioral patterns that may give cue to them that a seizure is about to take place. For this, you must select a dog that has a high dependency on its handler. Many dogs possess an innate ability to predict these episodes, once it is established that a dog has this ability, alert behaviors are encouraged and rewarded. These behaviors include pawing, barking and/or excessive licking. Golden retrievers seem to be high on the list for these dogs.

An example of someone who may need a seizure alert dog is someone who suffers from epilepsy. In the United States alone, 2 million people suffer from epilepsy. Service dogs give these people the freedom to be independent and function in their daily lives without fear of having an epileptic seizure. The training for a seizure alert dog who is accurate is two years including the basic foundation training. If you would like and/or need a dog sooner than this, you may consider getting and/or training a seizure response dog.

Seizure Response Dog: Similar to a seizure alert dog, a Seizure Response Dog aids in the safety of people who suffers from seizures. Unlike a seizure alert dog, the responsibility of a seizure response dog is not to warn of an impending seizure but to react to an ongoing seizure. A dog that is trained to respond to someone experiencing a seizure can do the following; seek out a person for help (be it a teacher, parent or friend), fetch medicine to treat said seizure, alert the public of their owners by barking (if a friend or family member is not around) provide comfort to their owner during the seizure, it an emergency button, or even break the fall of their own to avoid any head trauma. In some cases, if the person is in a wheelchair, the dog can pull the wheelchair to a safer location. This requires a dog to be strong and sturdy enough break their owners fall. A dog with hip, elbow, back or other joint issues would not be a good candidate for this type of work. When their owner is coming out of a seizure, they may retrieve their phone for them to call for help or bring medication to them.

Autism Support Dogs: Depending on the individual, a person or child on the autism spectrum experiences a wide variety of obstacles. A couple of these include but are not limited to; social isolation and/or wandering off. For children on the autism spectrum who have trouble connecting to peers at school or other social settings, the dog serves as a talking point as well as a familiar face and companion. This can give the child more independence and a better quality of life. Some children who have to deal with the trials of autism often wander off and can easily become lost. Autism Support Dogs are trained to keep their handler in the vicinity, and if they do run away, the dogs are trained to track them down and return them to their caregiver. Due to the fact that the dog must be able to focus on his/her handler at all times, they must possess the qualities of handler dependence and guardianship. Guardianship does not mean that the dog will protect the handler in an aggressive way, rather s/he will watch over them so that they do not hurt themselves or get lost. Some people on the autism spectrum often have episodes of self-destructive behavior such as; pulling their hair out, hitting themselves, or biting themselves or worse. During these episodes, the dog can be trained to stop their owner by pawing at their arms to interrupt the behavior. Another action the dog can perform during this time is to lay on top of their owner and sometimes lick their face in order to calm them down by providing deep-pressure therapy.

They can also be paired to children who suffer from fetal alcohol spectrum disorder. With similar symptoms, dogs are trained to interrupt repetitive behaviors. There is a wide variety of reasons someone could suffer from repetitive behaviors such as autism, obsessive-compulsive disorder, or even Tourette's syndrome. These behaviors can be subtle such as teeth grinding, picking at the skin, and nail-biting to much more extreme behavior like self-biting, banging one's head against an object, and repetitive self-hitting. As a whole, these behaviors are generalized as self-stimming. Many scientists believe that in children who suffer from autism, self-stimming provides their otherwise under a stimulated nervous system with the beta-endorphins it craves. Luckily, your service dog can be trained notice these behaviors attempt to stop them. To do this, you will need to present the dog with a repetitive behavior most common to you.

Emotional Support Dogs and Therapy Dogs: Unlike a service dog, an Emotional Support Dog offers companionship to those who suffer from emotional distress. You must have a letter from a licensed mental health professional expressing the need for your support dog. This letter will protect you under the Fair Housing Authority Act and the Air Carriers Act. It is important to be honest about this with yourself because if you can truthfully go on an airplane without your dog, you should. Airlines only allow one dog per flight. If you have bought a ticket for yourself and reserved a spot for your emotional support dog, this means a service dog must find a different flight. This service dog may serve as someone's guide dog, mobility dog, or another more severe disability. Most people with service dogs choose not to fly unless they absolutely need to, often times for medical reasons. Reasons such as flying to receive medical treatment or surgery. It is also important to note that a specific letter from a mental health professional is required to be shown at all airlines.

Although emotional support dogs are not allowed in public or protected by the Americans with Disabilities Act like service dogs are, they do have special clearance to places like hotels, airplanes, and housing that would otherwise not typically allow pets. Property owners can also ask to see a letter written by a mental health professional. A reasonable pet fee may apply depending on where you choose to apply to live.

A therapy dog's sole purpose is to go into hospital, orphanages and other establishments to bright the days of those there. They live with one person but not to better their quality of life. This means they are not protected under any act and do not have access to the public, airplanes or special privileges when it comes to housing. Some therapy dogs are purchased by orphanages or funeral homes by the owners so that they cheer up the residents and/or visitors.

Chapter 3: House Rules

Now that you've welcomed your new pup home, there are some basic rules we need to go over! Over the course of human history, dog and humans have served each other in many ways. In the earliest documented domestication, dogs were utilized as protectors and hunting partners. Tribes of people would intelligently tap into their dog's mental makeup and manipulate their instincts to better serve them. At the root of their mental makeup is their understanding and innate guidelines of pack structuring. We have all heard of the levels in which they design their packs; alpha, beta, omega, etc. Why do they require such a structure? Based on the proven fact, a unit will not survive without a system of hierarchy. More specifically, it will not survive without a leader. Through history, however, man has molded this in a way that serves them. Domestication created dogs that did not seek to be a leader. Instead, they craved one. Unfortunately, many who do not understand a domestic dog's mindset (especially one who would be perfect for service dog work) fail to be the leader and give structure that the dog needs. In this case, the dog (a dog who would otherwise be content having a confident leader) still being of the pack structuring mindset, will see their owner as unfit or equal to them and assume the role of leader themselves. At this point, the owner is aware of the issue but not the underlying cause. Many of these dogs develop anxieties when they take on the role of leader because they are uncomfortable in the position.

This can cause fearful, aggressive behavior. So how do you make sure you stay in control? You must have strict and consistent guidelines that your dog has to adhere to. Trust me, they will thank you and even love you more as their life guide and leader!

A lot of the time, with puppies *and* rescue dogs but *mostly* rescue dogs, their new owner make a huge mistake. They will take them home, and because they are new and often times have spent months in a kennel, their owners feel bad for them and thus give them everything under the sun. They are so excited to have a new puppy or dog that they go to the store and buy 50 dogs toys, lots of treats and then go home and let them up on the bed and furniture, etc. Now, I'm not saying you can't give your dog all this, but the way they get it is important. Think of it this way; imagine you grew up and everything was handed to you, you never had to work for money, you could go out wherever you'd like without asking permission, and never had to do any work around the house. How would you view money? Would you value it, or would you see it as a right and not a privilege? How do you think you would view your parents? Would you view them as respected and loved authority or would you see them as equals with no power over you? Most likely in this scenario, if they ever tried to reprimand you there would be an outburst. This is called spoiling, and I'm not sure when it became a positive word, but it creates monsters to both children and dogs.

Let's look at the other side of the spectrum; you have always worked for what you want, your parents are loving but firm, you must ask before doing whatever you'd like, and you do chores around the house for your allowance. In this scenario, your parents have made it clear they are in control and hold everything that you see of as value. You must either work for them to give you money or ask their permission to get/do something you want. The same is true with dogs. Like children, they want things, and if they can get them whenever they'd like, then you are of no importance to their needs and desires. Let's say you let your dog on your furniture, that's fine, and I'm not telling you that you can't. However, how they get up there is important. To understand this, you must see furniture as elevation, an elevation that you freely sit on without asking permission. In a dog's mind, elevation is power and ranking status. If they are able to climb up to your level of rank whenever they choose, do you really think they are going to take your commands seriously when they much rather investigate a smell? No, they will see you as an equal just as that spoiled child sees their parents as equals because they were given the ability to do what they like whenever they like. Some dogs even take it to the next level as to not let anyone on the furniture when they are on it. Believe it or not, all of these house rules will apply to when you are out in public. The same as a child who has a complete meltdown because they were told no in public. A dog that sees you as an equal and not a leader first will blow off commands seeing them as suggestions.

That being said, this is **rule number one:** NO furniture for the first week. After the first week, they are only allowed on the furniture when they ask and/or invited up. Most dogs will ask by placing their chin on the seat where they want to climb up on. I say no furniture for the first week because we want to make it very clear at first who is in charge to get off on the right foot. This will make your training sessions smoother, and you'll have to work less hard further down the road. It's okay if they get on the couch if you leave the room AS LONG AS they get off when you reenter.

Now, if by the second week you are allowing them to come up on the furniture when invited and they decide to start going up whenever they feel like it, correct them (I suggest leaving a short leash on them to guide them off of the couch) . If they continue to push this boundary, move them back to week one where they get no time on the furniture. This rule is especially important if you plan on having your dog sleep with you in the bed. The bed is like the King/Queen's throne to a dog. They must be invited up ONLY. Especially if you need them to do work at that location. If this work includes a grounding behavior (also known as deep pressure therapy) and you are worried you won't able to invite them up during a panic attack, don't fret. A dog can learn to become intellectually disobedient* in this situation where s/he will understand that they are only allowed up if invited or needed.

Rule number two: No "free-feeding." Traditionally free-feeding refers to the act of leaving food out for your dog to eat whenever s/he wishes. However, in this book, it also means feeding treats for no reason. Seems simple, but let's dive in a little deeper. Dogs not only view food as currency during training but they obviously also need it to survive just as you and I do. So it only makes sense that if we hold what is of importance to them, we become important. The more they must look to us to obtain what they desire, the more desirable we become to them. I would even suggest not having food bowls so that all of the food comes from you and training.

A dog that can eat whenever s/he wants will not value food. "Why would I work for that when I get it every morning and night for free every day?" – Your Dog. If your dog does not value food s/he will have little to no or less incentive to work for you. It's the same issue many people have with the welfare system in the United States. Depending on who you are, it lowers your incentive to work because you get a check in the mail right on schedule every month. Don't put your dog on welfare.

Later in this book, I will be asking you to set aside at least three, 15-minute sessions every day. As an example, if your dog eats three cups daily, you will split it up three ways and will have a cup of food to work with per session. (Plus jackpot rewards, but we will get into that later in the book) Doing this will send a simple message to your dog that he must earn his money(food) and if you make the work fun for him/her, you'll be in a beautiful and healthy relationship. This will also ensure that your dog is hungry and willing to work for his food. I love ribs, but if I eat a whole rack, you couldn't get me to eat one more bite. The same is true for dogs, if they are hungry they will be willing to work for the food. If they already had breakfast, the food probably isn't that enticing to them, and they won't want to work for it. In fact, on the days you take a rest from training your dog should fast. Don't worry, as long as they are regularly fed through training one day a week can actually be healthy for their digestive system!

Rule number three: Pick up their toys! It's okay if you were the person to go out and buy them the 50 toys they needed to have. However, just as it is important how they get up on the furniture and how they get their food, it is important how they get their toys.

In this chapter, we are talking about building a strong foundation for your growing relationship with your dog. Toys are a wonderful form of bonding, but this form of bonding can be less valuable to the dog if they are able to pick up, chew on, and play with their toys at free will. Playtime should have a start, and an end decided only by you. Just like training the play time should be kept short and fun. Tug-o-war is a great example of a bond building game. However, if they pick up a toy and bring it to you and you start to play... have they not just commanded you? Now you're being trained by your dog! Having your dog's toys out for them to pick up whenever they want is a lot like what happens with children with a lot of toys to play with. They start losing their value. But when Mom or Dad bring out a special toy that they are only allowed to play with when Mom or Dad bring it out, that toy becomes the most valuable toy even with 49 other toys laying around all around them.

Have a toy chest or box you can keep all their toys in and take out a toy to play with every day a few times a day. For example, you want to play tug-o-war, take the toy out and say to your dog, "Want to play?" or "Playtime!" or any phrase you'd like in order to signal to your dog the beginning of play. Play with them for 15-20 minutes and then take the toy and put it away. You will also need a phrase to signal the end of play time such as, "Game over." Or "No more." While playing tug-o-war, don't believe the myth that you should never let the dog win. Do you want to play a game you never win at? Probably not. It will not make them think they are higher ranking than you as long as you have correctly followed all of these rules. If anything, it will build their confidence, and they will see you as someone who built them up.

Rule number four: Stick together! The more time your dog spends with you, the better, especially while you are getting to know one another. Although you can't take your service dog with you everywhere just yet, it is important that while you are home that they be with you as much as possible. This will ensure they know all of your habitual patterns and will know exactly when something is wrong. As I have said before, dogs rely on routine and order of events to decide what is worth remembering. If you are with them all the time, this will paint a better picture for them of what is regular and irregular in your behavior. Later in the book we will discuss functional analysis* is regards to your dog's behavior. However, many people don't think about how dog's use the very same technique on us and that is why it's an effective tool when modifying a dog's behavior because they process information the same way. When a dog sees the behavior and what elicits it, such as someone with PTSD having a panic attack(behavior) when in an environment where people are over-crowded (what elicits it), s/he then responds without being told to do so in order to cease the behavior. The dog may have to be told what to do at first but will soon catch on when they see consistent tells of when the panic attack is going to happen. If the dog is not around his/her partner enough, they will not have a clear black and white reference to act upon.

This also brings us to the topic of work vs. task. We will talk more about this in the final chapter of this book, but I'd like to go over the difference between the two, so you can think of more examples on your own that apply to your specific disability and the importance of rule number four to you.

Work: A behavior or action a dog exhibits on their own in order to alert his/her owner of something.

Some dogs are trained to remind their owners to take medicine at a certain time. Hearing assistance dogs will notify their partner that there is someone at the door, or that the phone is ringing. This is also where the term intelligent disobedience comes into play. An example of this is, what we mentioned earlier, a dog is not allowed on the furniture but if their owner has a panic attack, they understand that that is prioritized above the house rules as an exception. Only then are they allowed on the bed. First, the dog may have to be told what to do in the situation, but they will quickly understand their role and perform their duty without guidance. Part of your dog's work is to be focused on you, time together solidifies this duty along with training and bonding exercises. More on that in the next chapter!

Task: A behavior or action a dog performs based on the command given by his/her owner in order to mitigate his/her Disability.

An example of this is someone in a wheelchair who has dropped his/her phone and is unable to pick it back up. They can then ask their dog to "get it" or "get the phone," and the dog will gently pick it up and hand it to them. Take a moment to think about the tasks you'd like to teach your dog! We will be covering hopefully at least one that you will need, including the one mentioned in this previous example.

Rule number five: Leash your dog. At least for the first week, you should keep a leash on your dog at all times. Not only will this aid in the rule of sticking together but it enables you to be able to nip and unwanted behaviors in the bud. Behaviors such as chewing, getting in the trash, jumping up on furniture, and jumping up on other people just to name a few. Correcting the unwanted behaviors is half the battle. It is important to also reward your dog for making the right decision in an instance where s/he had the opportunity to behave badly and chose not to. Which leads us to the rule inside this rule; keep treats on you or in accessible areas around your house for moments such as this. Just like children, dogs are always watching and learning. Don't miss the opportunity to reward those wanted behaviors!

Your dog will need to get used to the leash as if it's part of his/her body because they will be wearing it *a lot* during their training. At one point during the Public Access Test, you will need to drop your leash and then pick it up again. The dog must be aware that the leash is dropped and remain near you. This is a good time to practice desensitizing* your dog to this action so that it means nothing to them when you practice it in public.

Finally, **Rule Number Six:** Thresholds. Another rule that will serve you during your Public Access Test is how you and your dog walk through thresholds. This will be easier coupled with rule number five. When you walk through a doorway, it is important you walk through first and then your dog follows after you. This, of course, has the exception if your dog needs to pull your wheelchair through the doorway if need be. When s/he is not leashed, and you are walking outside of the house, you should walk through the door first and then "okay" your dog to cross the threshold. If your dog is crated (whether in the house or in the car) s/he should also not burst out of the crate when you open the door. To counter this, you can open the gate of the crate slowly and if s/he tries to push through, quickly shut the door. The idea is similar to walking on the leash (which we will address in a later chapter). Your dog has a self-serving agenda (in this case to get out of the crate on his time) and it's your responsibility to redirect their focus on to you. If s/he is focused on getting out of the crate, s/he is not focused on you. You may have to repeat shutting the door multiple times before s/he is waiting quietly for your "free" command. This switch in focus brings us to our next chapter.

Chapter 4: Engagement Training

When most people think about training their dog they think about the obvious sit, down, and come. Many people assume if they teach their dog how to sit, they will sit when told and if they didn't sit they are either stubborn or didn't hear them. While there are stubborn dogs (which by the way are difficult to train but make very obedient dogs once trained properly), many dogs simply aren't interested in what you're asking them, and on a larger scale, aren't interested in you. Dogs are living breathing animals with desires and a brain operating on free will just like you and I. They are not robots you can program one time and then expect them to maintain any level of training that you don't routinely practice. Like us, they require reoccurring mental stimulation, and it should be fun! If it isn't fun, we lose interest. If your dog is allowed to play alone, then s/he can gain independence away from you, and you will not have the level of focus required by a service dog. Activities such as running around with a ball, swimming, chewing on a bone, or anything that is self-rewarding can take away from the bond and engagement you are trying to build.

To reiterate, your service dog will need to be completely focused on you in public, this is part of his/her work. Distractions including people calling him/her to their attention, other dogs, squirrels, certain smells, etc., could compromise your dog's duty to mitigate your disability. Imagine if your prosthetic leg detached and ran off to investigate another leg. You'd fall.

So how do you demonstrate value to your dog, making you more interesting and important than that obnoxious individual that's whistling and clicking at your dog to get their attention? Engagement training! These games I am about to share with you will teach your dog how to focus, which will come in handy when you start to teach them their obedience and tasks. We will discuss this more in depth later in this chapter. For now, we need to charge the mark*!

Dogs see the world like flipping through a picture book whereas, humans see life more like a played out movie. Highlights of the dog's day are stored in these photo books, so s/he can remember them. Every time we mark a behavior with a reward or reprimand, the dog "takes a picture" of that moment and stores it in their brain book. We can harness this thought process by creating a noise (such as a clicker) or saying a word that will be positively or negativity associated. A big rule of thumb here is to *never* say your marker word unless you plan on paying your dog. How would you like it if your boss said he had money for you and then only gave you a high five?

Charging the mark: As stated, a mark can be in the form of a clicker, whistle, cluck, or word. Personally, I use the word, "Yes!" but you can use whatever you'd like. For the purposes of explaining, I will be using *click*.

- Ratio out 1/3rd of your dog's daily intake. If you plan on doing more than three sessions that day, fraction it out accordingly (5 sessions 1/5th, 6 sessions 1/6th, etc.) We want your dog to be hungry and willing to focus on what you have!

- Have your clicker ready or your throat cleared!

- Bring your dog out on a leash to a quiet area with minimal to no distractions. I suggest a room in your house or the backyard to begin with. Later we will add distractions but for now, let's make it easy for them.

- Start the session by saying a phrase to signal to your dog that a training session has started. "Let's go to work" is a common one but it can be anything you'd like.

- Have him/her in front of you with treats in your pocket (I suggest buying a treat pouch to make your life easier).

- *Click* and reward. Repeat. Again. Do it some more. Soon the treat will be able to come at any length of time after the click, however, for now, we need to make it crystal clear to your dog that the **mark (click) = the reward**. Picture the click as the shutter on your dog's brain camera collecting highlights/pictures of that session. To make this connection the food MUST come simultaneously with the mark.

- The end goal of this practice should be your dog whipping their head around every time they hear their mark.

- This may take about 6 sessions. If your dog is not CONSISTENTLY whipping their head around when they hear the mark do not continue.

- ALWAYS end on a good note. Reward the last click with a jackpot (a larger amount of food or food with higher value to your individual dog such as roast beef, cheese, hotdogs, etc.)

- Make it clear to your dog that the session is over by saying a concluding phrase. Many people say, "All done" or "Finished."

Name Recognition: In this chapter, we will discuss many different ways to teach your dog how to learn and build focus on you. This is a great starting point. Your dog's name should be like a bell for them to listen for further instructions. Too many people say it without meaning thus, making their name a background noise. If your dog's name means nothing to them, most likely they won't react to it when it is most important to. In the same token, many people make a negative association with their dogs name by using it to reprimand them. This creates avoidance when they hear their name. In order to cause a positive association with your dog's name, we must make it a highlight for them. How do we do that? You guessed it! Marking their name!

- Start the same way you did with charging the mark and have him/her on leash. Use the same area you used in the previous session. (Every time you add something new, you should pair it with something old).

- Say your starting phrase.

- Next, say your dog's name and wait for them to look at you. DO NOT repeat your dog's name, this will only make your marker less clear, and they will become further desensitized to their name.

- As soon as they look at you, *click* and reward. At this point, your dog knows that the marker = the reward, this means you can now take your time getting the treat to his/her mouth. But the marker MUST come simultaneously with the desired behavior.

- If they don't look at you right away take a few peppy steps back or lightly pop their leash to get their attention.

- Use the phrase you chose for closing the session once you are all out of treats.

- If after a few sessions they are still not immediately responding to their name, use whatever technique (trotting backward or popping their leash) that worked previously in unison with their name. For instance, if popping the leash worked for you, you can pop the leash and say their name. As a rule of thumb when testing progression, three old then one new. Three times popping in unison with their name, one without. Do this a few times until consistent.

- End with a jackpot!

- Signal the end with your closing phrase.

Food chasing/follow the leader: Now it's time they start to really engage! This exercise will help develop their luring skills. Later in this book, we will take more about luring when we go over obedience. For now, all you need to know is the skill does not come as naturally as you think. This exercise will also make it clear to them that they will always get rewarded as long as they keep trying! How sweet.

- Begin the session in a distraction-free environment. S/he should be on leash.

- Signal the start of your session using your chosen phrase.

- Hold the food in your hand with a closed fist so they cannot snatch it from you.

- Start to move your hand away from the dog's face by backing up and luring them along with you.

- After a few steps, *click* and open your hand giving the treat to him/her.

- Continue this but create increasing more difficult puzzles. For instance, at first, you may just have them follow your hand for a long period of time.

- Increase the difficultly even further by having them follow your hand onto objects like boxes or step ladders. Reward them for efforts and jackpot successes.

- Another difficulty, believe it or not, is to let them follow your hand in a circle so that they spin around. Take it slow and reward effort (half turns).

- Have fun and be creative with this. See how long your dog will try to get the food from you and reward just before that. Create duration in increments, thus building confidence and confirming you are building them up.

- End the session on a good note, jackpot, and give your concluding phrase!

Targeting Game: This will be a fun and very important game for your service dog and you! Targeting is going to help you later in this book when we start teaching tasks since it is the building block to most of their foundations. Once you have your pup following your hand, this will be a piece of cake.

- Begin your session like any other.

- With an empty hand reach out in front of your dog about 6-12 inches from their face, so it's clear if they show the hand attention.

- Once they show any kind of attention to your hand, *click* and reward.

- Then ask for more but not rewarding the previously accepted behavior. If you have done the rest of the games correctly, s/he should not give up but instead push harder.

- Wait for him/her to touch the hand, *click* and jackpot the positive progression.

- If you are having difficulties with step four and/or five, try placing a piece of food underneath your thumb to entice your dog to investigate. Once they do, *click* and release the hidden food from your hand. Repeat this three times and then on the fourth repetition, no food hidden but they still get a click and are rewarded from your other hand. This troubleshooting usually doesn't take long.

- Let's dive deeper into jackpots. So far, you've established what the jackpot is to your dog. Fortunately, dog's like to gamble and find it exciting and fun. Once your dog is consistently touching your hand, let them do it a few times before your reward. It's the same reason people go to slot machines. They are happy to pull that lever all day spending a fortune for the *chance* that they may hit the jackpot. Vary the times you do it. In other words, don't do it on the fourth rep every time, mixing it up will create that exciting factor for them. This will also help you in the future when we start weaning them off of getting paid for everything.

- Remember to stop when they want to continue. This way you're leaving them wanting more. Making them even more eager for the next session.

Adding distractions: Now that your dog is successfully engaged with you, we can now add small distractions. Consider what you will run into out in public and incorporate that into the environment you have been consistently training in. For example, ask a friend or family to mimic behaviors the public may do like clapping, whistling, clicking their tongue, etc. Even with a service dog vest, many people will be oblivious to the importance of your dog's attention on you. All you can do is accept it and prepare as best as you can.

- Begin as you would for any session and on leash.

- Start off with no distractions and say your dog's name, *click* and reward.

- Next, create the distraction. Have a friend or family member clap their hands once, and when the dog puts their attention on them say their name and when they look at you *click* and jackpot the progress.

- Don't worry if they don't look right away, it may take time. Just remember not to repeat yourself.

- Once they are consistently redirecting their attention from the clap to you, switch it up and have your helper whistle or cluck.

- One big distraction for dogs is when people crouch down on their level in an inviting fashion. Chances are you will run into a few people who feel it is okay to do this to a strange dog let alone a working service dog.

- Take baby steps in this environment and then after a few sessions of consistent success, try this on a walk. The biggest distractions dogs have is their nose!

Confidence Building Games: Another way to build a bond with your dog is to be their leader. I mean this in the sense that you build them up. The more right answers you have and the more they associate their confidence reaching new levels, the more attached they will become to you. I once was assigned to a chocolate Labrador named Drake who was very timid at first. My immediate thought was that Drake would not do well in a public environment. He couldn't walk without slinking, he was underweight from stress, and if you gave him a command, he would freeze up and become paralyzed with fear – all the things I warn you against when selecting a service dog. (Do not take this story as an exception to the adorable petrified dog you saw at the shelter. Drake was a special case and needed professional help).

I decided against my better judgment that Drake deserved more. Even if we had placed him in a pet home, his quality of life would be poor. So I gave him a two-week probation, if I did not see any improvement over the course of two weeks, he would be washed out as a pet. I began spending time going on walks with him and luring him into his obedience without giving any commands. These were just simple engagement exercises. He was happier but still very doubtful of himself. He would give up easily when following food in my hand and walk back to his crate to isolate himself. Little by little, I was rewarding him for touching my hand, then pushing my hand. When he was comfortable with that I would step back and if he followed he got a jackpot! Drake was starting to like this game. He was good at it! He started to request to play the game he was so skilled at. He thought about it constantly and his mood improved when he played these food chasing games. His tail was up he was bouncing and, in general, a noticeably different, happier dog. I decided to make commands something fun for him that he could be proud of.

To erase his stigma about commands, I got a long wooden broom and placed it on the floor. I lured him (his favorite game) over the broom, and at first, he hesitated but then made the leap. He had reached a new personal best! I let him do this a few times as I watched the pride grow inside him. Once he was really good at it, I added the word, "jump." Drake was now learning that obedience can be fun! I began raising the broom slightly at an angle so that he could choose any height he wanted, but I kept the food I was luring him with close to me (and the highest part of the broom jump). He started to become more confident as he decided to get closer to the treat to receive it faster. Now he was jumping knee high! I then raised the broom again so that he could only jump knee high. This change in visual daunted him for a short while, but with encouraging words, he made the leap and happily took the treat. In no time knee high height was nothing to him. Now it was time to get serious. I raised the broom so slightly each time he jumped it until it reached a point where he began to doubt himself again. He was right to doubt himself, how was he supposed to jump a broom above his eye-level at a standstill. Drake knew one thing, I hadn't let him down once, and he had succeeded every time. He studied the height for about twenty seconds and then took a literal leap of faith. I quickly lowered the broom as he leaped over it ensuring that he completely cleared it. If he had tried to jump that height from where he was standing, he would have failed. However, Drake landed on the other side and did not even care about receiving his reward! He exploded with excitement and began spinning in circled wagging his tail and licking me. I offered him his treat, and he took it then continued to rejoice. The next time we tried it at that level, he didn't hesitate at all, and I again lowered the broom.

After this exercise and many lessons in obedience, he was my best service dog! I could bring him anywhere in public, his attention was completely on me, and his head and tail were always carried high. He now pranced when he walked instead of slinking. He went from hiding in his crate to isolate himself to following me everywhere and anywhere off leash, outside, and interested in everything I was doing. He was constantly seeking ways he could be involved because everything we did together built him up! My point for telling this story is again not to urge you to pick a dog that needs rehabilitation because the truth is, I don't have Drake's history on why he came to me as a shell of himself, and there could be many reasons. Some dogs may not bounce back like Drake did, and this could lead to a lot of frustration during your training. My point of telling you this story is to illustrate the power of confidence building and engagement training and the impact it can have on the relationship between you and your dog.

Do you think Drake had every encountered someone spending that time with him and doing those seemingly weird exercises with him? No, most likely not. However, he became addicted to it. He didn't what we were doing, "yeah, mom asks me to do weird things like jump over brooms but I'm great at it!" the truth is, the more odd and peculiar things you show your dog the more confident they become. For instance, there's no real reason why your dog should ever have to balance on a fire hydrant, that's strange, but it will prepare them for strange things in life. The more out of the ordinary your dog's life is, the more new experiences won't give them pause!

One great way to get started with this is by using agility equipment. Agility is a great team sports for you and your dog to do together. If you're unable to fully do agility courses just using the equipment is good enough. Obstacles such as the A-frame, teeter totter, catwalk and of course jumps, are a fantastic way to introduce asking your dog for strange behaviors. All of these require balance and concentration so success with them will be rewarding for your dog and build their confidence!

Teeter Totter: The teeter-totter (or see-saw) is a fantastic way to build your dog's confidence. The balance mixed with a moving surface poses a challenge for most dogs and thus creates the perfect opportunity to boost their self-esteem.

- Start with your opening phrase so that your dog knows it is a time to solve a problem and learn.

- Lure your dog with food onto the low part of the teeter totter. (The part that is on the ground)

- *Click* and reward as soon as they touch it.

- Encourage them to climb further onto it until they have all four paws on the obstacle. Jackpot!

- Next reward them for steps (big or small) towards the top. Stop at the middle and jackpot them.

- When s/he is noticeably comfortable at this height, move the board with your hand in a controlled, subtle manner. Do not move it too fast or too far down.

- If your dog jumps off, simply have them climb back up again.

- Just get them used to hanging out in the middle and having the board move.

- Once they are comfortable with this, slowly move the board down and watch your dog's reaction to this.

- Use your judgment as to when you should stop, *click,* and reward them for staying on.

- Your goal is to move the board all the way to the ground slowly and gradually increase speed.

- Once your dog is comfortable with a relatively fast speed, lure them to the other side of the board so that they are the ones pushing it down.

- Lure them slowly and reward them as soon as they make the board move.

- Soon your dog will be sprinting across the teeter totter!

Please do not progress further in the book until you can confidently grab your dog's attention and keep it. Keep one game to a session but do a few different games a day. This will keep it exciting for your pup.

Chapter 5: Obedience

Congratulations on being one step closer to this exciting journey with your service dog! Before we start with your first command, let's discuss the general guidelines of teaching and maintaining these lessons.

- Never say your marker word (or click your clicker) without following it with a reward.

- Do not give a command you cannot reinforce.

- When you teach something new pair it with something old.

- Do not progress until your dog is one hundred percent crystal clear in the previous step.

- Try not to repeat yourself, it only confuses the dog and makes them tune you out.

- When you give your marker, your dog should remain in position to receive the reward.

- Keep the sessions short (10-15 mins).

- When in doubt, go back to the last step your dog excelled at.

- If you find yourself frustrated, end on a good note and revisit the lesson later. Being frustrated will only deteriorate the communication between you and your dog.

You and your service dog in training have come on a very rewarding and stress-free journey so far when it comes to engagement and confidence training. It is important that both of these are strong because they are about to be tested. As you ask more from your dog, s/he will much likely to get pressured. You will notice it when s/he refuses food, when s/he freezes up, or if s/he finds more interest in other things around you during the training. If this happens, bring your dog back to the basics of engagement games. Make interacting with you a game again. When you go back to your obedience or task training, start slower and ease into what your dog was having trouble with.

This is not a time-sensitive issue, and all dogs learn at different speeds. Accepting this will actually make your training start speeding up. Recognize that your baby (three-year-old human child mentality) needs baby steps and you are his/her leader. Set micro goals for your dog and reward them for achieving those goals. If you are having trouble teaching him/her to spin, for example, reward him/her for following your hand first. Next set a goal that s/he will follow your hand behind them and just reward for their neck bending in the right direction. Soon your baby's steps will turn into one fluid motion and eventually your dog will be spinning rapidly! Baby steps should be looked at on a large scale and small. On a small scale, we have a large amount of small steps leading up to one action. On a larger scale, however, each new action your dog learns (and learns properly) will help him or her become a well-rounded and obedient service dog. To bridge this engagement obedience gap, we will use a game that includes both but is heavy on the engagement side. Baby steps! Or should I say, puppy steps!

Walking on a Loose Leash: When you are out in public, your dog must stay by your side (unless a task called for them to briefly leave your side). The beginning of this process may not make sense to you, but the idea is to give your dog a crystal clear understanding that they are to follow you and when on a leash they are not in charge of where they go (like follow the leader). This will come in great handy when you take your Public Access Test.

- At first, you will need no treats for this exercise.

- Hook your pup up to about a five-foot leash.

- Let them hit the end of the leash (with you holding the end of the leash giving them the full length) and soon as they do, switch directions sharply.

- The idea behind this is that the dog will think s/ he is the leader until you change directions surprising him/her, giving no other option but to follow you.

-

- Make sure you are walking in a straight line so that it is black and white to your dog what is correct and incorrect.

- **Troubleshooting:** If your dog refuses to follow you when you change direction, wait them out. Say nothing to them but keep steady pressure on the leash. Remain calm, and eventually, they will concede. This requires patience. Reward them with a treat once they comply.

- **Troubleshooting:** If your dog is not walking the line (you seem to be walking in a circle), when you change direction do it in opposite direction of where your dog is pulling.

- Once they start to not hit the end of the leash, start randomly switching direction. Don't walk the same amount of steps each time. (Your dog will predict turns pretty quickly) Surprising them will make them believe they have to keep their focus on you to know where they have to go.

- As they progress slowly, take the leash in foot by foot until they are right next to you. Chances are you will get there fairly fast with consistency.

- To make it easier, at this point choose one side you want your dog to be in the majority of the time when walking.

Sit: One of the most basic commands you can teach, sit will be most useful when you're standing in line. Besides this, it is a great first command to teach your dog. Remember the luring games we taught your dog? This will now come into play!

- For this, you will need treats.

- Begin with your starting phrase.

- Have your dog in front of you on a leash.

- Hold the food in your fist and bring it to their nose, using the food as a magnet lure your dog's nose up so that they are looking up. This will create an uncomfortable position for your dog's neck to hold for a long period of time and to make up for the annoying position they will sit in order to straighten out their spine.

- As soon as their butt hits the floor, *click* and release the food.

- Repeat a few times, remembering to jackpot progress.

- In the beginning, you will be rewarding them every time.

- Reward good intentions! Once you've don't a few repetitions, your dog may start offering you the behavior you've been practicing. If they give you the behavior without you asking *(while you are teaching the behavior)* jackpot them! This means you have their full attention and they are digesting what you are communicating to them.

- Finish on a good note and a jackpot and use your closing phrase.

After they are predictably sitting without you having to lure them, add the word!

- Hold the treat in your hand normally, if they try to go for the treat do *not* pull your hand away. Some dogs may see this as a game, like the luring game.

- Next, say the word *sit* and wait for them to do so. Count to about 5 and if they are still having trouble understanding what you are asking slowly move your hand with the treat towards them as if you're going to lure them. Once they see that picture, they will realize you are asking them to sit. Let their butt hit the ground and immediately *click*.

- The goal is to not lure at all. Most of the time the dog will stop waiting for you to lure and just beat you to it by sitting thus obtaining the treat faster.

- Once s/he is proficient with the sit, then you can start to vary your rewards and stop paying for good intentions. In other words, only pay when you say "sit."

- After this, start asking for "sit" while you are out on walks and jackpot the progress.

Down: One of your most used commands will be down. You'll likely use it anytime you go to sit down anywhere or are at a counter somewhere for an extended period of time.

- Begin as you would any lesson with a new command.

- We are going to be using luring again!

- Make sure they are in standing position. A dog that learns how to down from a sit will only understand how to down if they are already in a sit. Have what is called, poor proprioception and we will talk about it in just a minute.

- This time, bring the treat from their nose to the ground. The more they try to get the treat from you, the better. So make sure they are hungry!

- Don't move your hand away and don't talk to your dog. You'll only distract him or her as s/he tries to figure out how to get your hand open.

- S/he will compensate for the uncomfortable position by lowering their body to straighten their spine. Once their butt and elbows hit the ground, *click* and reward.

- **Troubleshooting:** If your dog is giving up easily, start rewarding interest in the treat. This way your dog will not lose hope, and you are telling him his on the right track.

- **Troubleshooting:** If your dog is staying on task but is having a hard time figuring out this puzzle, you can reward him/her for their efforts by rewarding in increments.

- Have patience. This is not a race and the more time you give your dog to figure out the problem the more s/he will retain it.

- End your session the way you would any other, on a good note and with a jackpot reward!

Earlier we mentioned proprioception. This is the awareness and perception of the body's position and its movements. Most dogs have poor proprioception, hence they may have the inability to generalize "sit" as an action that can be done anywhere from any position. These different combinations have to be taught.

Troubleshooting: If your dog freezes and seemingly "forgets" looking at you with a blank stare, simply move three feet to the left or right and try again. This resets the dog's brain since they don't multitask well. It may sound strange, but walking them three feet left or right is a task for them which means when they have to switch back to the actual task at hand their mind is fresh. This also important to do in order to test if a dog is listening or just in auto-pilot.

Building Duration: Now your dog knows "sit" and "down" proficiently! Now it's time to build duration so that they aren't expecting a treat right away every time you mark the correct behavior. Full disclosure: this requires patience!

- Begin the session as you would any for "sit."

- Tell your dog to *sit*.

- Once his/her butt hits the floor immediately *click*.

- Wait one whole "Mississippi."

- Reward the dog in position.

- **Troubleshooting:** If your dog gets up from the position, freeze as if you're a robot dispensing treats and your dog's action of getting out of position broke you. Keep a closed fist and remain like this until your dog goes back into his/her sit. Once they go back into their sit, you may resume giving the treat. Do *not* repeat the command and do *not* repeat the marker.

- Incrementally increase the time between the marker and the treat. Once you have built up a good amount of time, vary the duration. Dogs can count! If you do it four seconds every time in the same fashion, they will get up on the fifth second.

- End the session on a good note and jackpot any great progress!

Do this for down as well! Once s/he is proficient in both sit and down with duration it will be time to move on from this foundation and turn it into a command!

Stay: Most of the time you are going to be tethered to your partner. However, if for whatever reason you need to keep them in a stay while you walk away, you may tie them to an object or have a friend or family member hold the leash. If this is the case, you'll want your dog to have a bulletproof stay.

- Begin your session in your distraction-free environment!

- Have a leash on your dog.

- Ask your dog to *down*. If it takes him a while, mark and reward it. You cannot build a strong stay on a weak foundation.

- If he downs immediately say, *stay*.

- With the leash loose, walk a foot or so to the left or right. If s/he stays in position, *click* and reward. You may say "free" to indicate that s/he is allowed to get up. Pair "free" with a gentle tug on the leash so they understand what you are trying to communicate to them.

- **Troubleshooting:** Alternatively, if you say "stay" and your dog breaks position, simply say "no" and bring them back to the area they were in and they should down on their own. If they don't down on their own, it is okay to repeat the command "down" but not "stay."

- Repeat step six until they comply and stay.

- Keep the duration no longer than you had built off your down before. You may say "good" as a bridge word to let your dog know they are on the right track to getting a reward. When you say "good," say it in a soothing calm voice that invokes calmness in them. Dogs read our energy, if we are hyped they get hyped. If we are calm, they will match our energy. That being said, reassure your dog by saying, "goooood." Almost as if you are petting them with your voice. (Never use your bridge word or marker unless you are going to reward your dog)

- Repeat these repetitions in various locations in your distraction-free environment for about ten minutes. This is one of the hardest commands your dog will learn because it takes concentration and consciousness to suppress the impulse to break position

Let's talk for a minute about why you don't want to use your bridge word or marker unless you are going to reward your pup and how you're going be able to apply it to the rest of your dog's life. As stated before, dogs process information according to the order of events to predict what will happen next. This is called Functional Analysis, a simple math problem you can remember to better communicate to them in the future is A + B = C. Also known as the ABCs of behavior.

A: Antecedent

B: Behavior

C: Consequence

Let's take the example of what is happening in your dog's brain when s/he hears the marker word. If you've been consistent, one click equals one reward (big or small). Imagine you work all week (your dog's action) and every Friday, your boss tells you he has a check for you (click), and you get your paycheck (reward) consistently every time. Then imagine one week your boss says he has a paycheck for you (click) and you don't get a paycheck. The first time you're probably a little upset, but you continue to do your job. Since then, every Friday your boss continues to tell you he has a check for you, but sometimes he's lying and sometimes it's your regular pay. It's the same premise behind The Boy Who Cried Wolf. Eventually, your boss saying, "I have your paycheck" will mean nothing to you and you will just start waiting for your check instead of paying any attention to your boss. It is important for your dog to trust you.

This is different than the varied reward/jackpot system. The varied reward system is designed to make your dog work harder because s/he gets bonuses for working harder making them excited to work.

Take the example of the command we just went over. You ask your dog to *down* and stay your dog does this successfully (A for Antecedent), and you *click* (B for Behavior), and your dog receives the reward in a reasonable time (C for Consequence). Now imagine they get A and B but not always C. Your cue (behavior) will start to mean less to the dog making it harder for you to communicate to them what they are doing correctly in the future.

This is why dogs continue to bark at mailmen, think about it. If A + B = C 100% of the time, they will keep the behavior. If A + B ≠ C 100% of the time they will throw the behavior out.

Antecedent: The mailman comes to the door.

Behavior: Your dog barks at them.

Consequence: The mailman leaves.

Your dog doesn't know he's leaving because he's done delivering the mail, he believes his barking is sending him away based on the order of events. If you were to take away or change the consequence s/he would stop the behavior.

Recall: This is one of the most important commands for any dog to know in case of an emergency. Most of the time your service dog will be tethered to you or by your side but every dog needs freedom, and if you decide to take your dog to the park or other public area, it is imperative that they have a bulletproof recall. It could save their life.

- Prepare yourself with a long line (about 20-30 feet will do)

- Since the majority of the time, you'll have to call your dog to you is when they aren't paying attention to you, wait until they are sniffing the ground or looking away about three feet away from you.

- Say your dog's name immediately followed by, "come" or "here." Simultaneously with the command, gently reel him/her into you.

- As soon as s/he gets to you, *click* and reward.

- This should be a high energy game. You never want to call your dog to you to reprimand them, ever. This command should *always* be positive.

- The better your dog gets, the more distance and distraction you can create.

- Try not to make your dog down-stay somewhere in order to call them. This does not only defeats the purpose of recalling away from distraction (because the dog's focus is already on you) but it can harm your stay command since it is freshly learned. You should stick to one command per session, especially when learning a new command.

You should be the only person ever giving your dog commands. That being said, let's play a fun game I like to call, "Pass the Puppy." This game will ensure your dog will come back to you if ever enticed by another person in public. You will need to find a friend or family member to help you.

- You hold the end of the long line and your reward should be of higher value than the person helping you.

- Stand about six feet from your helper.

- Your helper should crouch down and offer food, petting or just praise. The helper should not say the dog's name or give the dog any commands, they should also not actually ever give the dog any food. To entice the dog to come to them they can whistle, click their tongue, pat their leg, clap their hands, baby talk, etc.

- Let your dog investigate them.

- When you're ready, call your dog to you as you normally would *with* the leash pop and guide them to you. Incorporate the leash guidance even if your dog has moved past this step. Remember, when you add something new, supplement it with something old/familiar.

- When your dog gets to you, *click* and jackpot them. Give lots of praise but only mark as soon as they get to you. This means if your marker is "yes" do not say "yes" again to praise them.

- Create distance between you and the helper.

- **Troubleshooting:** If your dog has trouble leaving the attention of your helper, lower the level of attention the helper gives and raise your reward.

Once s/he is performing his/her recall well with limited distraction, try it without the leash guidance but still hold onto the end. Here are the increments you should progress with this command. Keep in mind, you will practice each step until proficient. This may take a few sessions to get down this list.

- **At the very beginning:** Short distance, leash guidance simultaneously with command, reel them in.

- Create more distance, simultaneous leash guidance, reel them in.

- Full long line distance, simultaneous leash guidance, reel them in.

- Short distance, simultaneous leash guidance, do **not** reel them in.

- Longer distance, simultaneous leash guidance, do **not** reel them in.

- Longest distance, simultaneous leash guidance, do **not** reel them in.

- Short distance, no leash movement at all.

- **Troubleshooting:** Remember, if at all during these steps your dog gets confused just go back to the last step s/he was proficient at.

- Longer distance, no leash movement at all.

- Longest distance, no leash movement at all.

- **Troubleshooting:** If during your progression in which you are at a step that requires less leash involvement; your dog gets confused, use the leash to clarify what you are asking.

- Now it is time to add even more distance. Drop the leash, and let them drag it. Call them as you normally would. When they get to you, *click* and jackpot. Give lots of praise.

- **Troubleshooting:** If your dog isn't letting you create distance by following you around, give it time. Just like children they will get bored and try to find something more interesting to focus on. *This* is the perfect opportunity to show them that you are more interesting than anything else around.

- **Troubleshooting:** if your dog doesn't respond to you right away or gets confused, go to the end of the line and reel them in. Never go to the dog.

- Bring in a friend to help play, "Pass the Puppy."

- Short distance with leash assistance.

- Short distance without leash assistance.

- Longer distance with leash assistance.

- Longer distance without leash assistance.

- Longest distance with leash assistance.

- Longest distance without leash assistance.

- Next, start recalling your dog when they are on their way to the helper.

- Start when they just leave you and give leash assistance.

- Then wait to call them until they are half way to the helper. Use the leash.

- Then call them right before they get to the helper. This is will most difficult for a dog. Once a dog has gone past 50% of the way towards a distraction their attention is harder to achieve. This is why we practice for this.

- Use your own judgment on how much distraction you should start out with and progress accordingly. Each pup will be different.

- Start practicing on walks.

- Short distances with leash assistance.

- Long distances with leash assistance.

- Have your dog walking on a loose leash and have your helper try to entice your dog. If they start to walk towards them, call them back as we did in steps 22-25. If your dog doesn't bother going towards them and refocuses on you, jackpot them and give them lots of praise!

Tip: Use lots of different helpers. Not always the same person.

Attention Heeling: First used by military and police working dogs, an attention heel was taught to keep the dogs focus on the handler as they walked through a crowd so that their more reactive dogs would not get distracted and agrees towards fast motions or disorderly but non-threatening civilians. Today it is used by a wide variety of people who want more control over their dogs when walking by distractions such as traffic, other animals, food, etc. This is meant to be for short times when you are walking by a distraction, not for an entire long walk.

- Start with your opening phrase.

- Begin by luring your dog (with leash guidance) into the heel position. There are a few ways you can do this. You can either lure them past your leg from the front and then back towards you into position on your side with their feet in line with yours or, you can have them circle behind you via the opposite side of your choosing and finish in the heel position.

- Never cross body feed. This means if your dog is heeling on your left, you will feed with your left hand and click with your right (if you use a clicker). Crossbody feeding promotes your dog forging ahead of you to get closer to the reward, which defeats the purpose of the heel.

- Your feeding hand should be in line with your hip and adjacent to it. If your dog is taller than your hip, you can raise the height accordingly.

- Begin to build duration by withholding the treat. Use your bridge word "good" to encourage them to stay in position.

- Once your dog is getting into position without being lured, it is time to start moving.

- First, jackpot one step. Then two. Continue to add until you can do five steps and then start to reward at random.

- If your dog looks away, pop the leash to get his/her attention. Your dog will understand this popping of the leash if you followed the steps for walking on a loose leash correctly.

- Begin adding turns and reward him/her for even half turns. Remember baby steps!

- At the end of each lesson give your closing phrase!

- Have a helper stand stationary near you and just reward your pup getting into position around another person. Then walk around the person.

- Get two helpers and practice your heeling in a figure eight motion around them.

- Next, have them walk by you while you are getting your pup into position.

- This time, walk past each other and keep your pup's attention.

- Remember, you control the speed at which you walk. It is easy to find ourselves matching our dog's speed when we should really be making them match ours. To do this, you can hyper slow down your pace and reward more frequently. Do not reward more frequently if you are following your dog's pace.

Free Shaping: Free shaping is something we will be using a lot in this book. It is different from luring. With luring, you are guiding the dog into the behavior or position you desire. With free shaping, you are letting the dog figure out how to get the desired behavior on their own. This is done by rewarding incremental good intentions. This is a great way for a dog to learn because it boosts creativity, confidence, and solidifies the behavior better than if they were lured. To practice this, we will use the command, "place" as an example.

Place: Place is a good command to have for your dog when you are at home and need them to go lay down. Place can be anything from a blanket on the floor, to a dog bed, or a crate. It is also useful when you bring your dog to work.

- Start by giving your opening phrase.

- Have a towel or dog bed out on the floor anywhere in the room.

- If this is a new object, your dog may naturally investigate it. That being said, I suggest using a towel to start out with (you can always change it to a different object later.)

- You may sit or stand. If your dog pays any attention to the towel, *click* and let them come to you to get the reward.

- **Troubleshooting:** This does require some patience and time, however, remember that distance can make it easier or harder. If your dog is spending time near you trying to figure out how to get the treat, move the towel closer to you so that you have a better chance of your dog paying attention to the towel.

- **What constitutes as attention?** Looking, sniffing, and stepping on it all lead to the goal; which is to lay down on it. Try to avoid rewarding biting as this will cause your dog to go down a different path away from the goal you are trying to achieve.

- Incrementally and consistently reward behavior that is in the direction of the goal you are trying to achieve. Remember to jackpot any major progression such as; they have been being rewarded for looking at the towel, and they decide to step towards it. That calls for a jackpot! Or they have been stepping on paw on it and all of the sudden they put two paws on it. Jackpot!

- Continue this and once they are offering you your end goal, start moving the towel around to different areas. This will build your dog's proprioception and solidify the command. If s/he gets confused, start rewarding good intentions again. If need be, move the towel back to the original spot, so s/he doesn't get too confused and then only move it a foot or two in one direction.

Break: Another example of free shaping includes waiting for teaching moments. Two of the easiest behaviors to free shaping are defecating and urinating. You can create two commands for this (one for #1 and one for #2). Due to both of these commands having the same steps we will use the term "break."

- First, you must have a general understanding of your dog's schedule of when s/he needs to go to the bathroom. This will give you the best chance of being prepared so that you can be consistent.

- Bring your dog out to go to the bathroom and make sure you have your reward on you if you use a clicker have it with you as well.

- When your pup does the desired behavior, *click* at the finish of the action. If you have charged your mark correctly and consistently, your dog should whip his/her head around and beeline towards you. Feed him/her upon reaching you.

- Once s/he is going to the bathroom sooner each time you let him/her out, begin adding the word. In this case, I will use "break."

- Bring your dog out to go to the bathroom, say *break* and wait for him/her to "go." *Click* and jackpot. Eventually, the word will preface the action, and your dog will associate the word with the action.

Free Shaping Box: you've done this with place but as stated before, the more you ask your dog to do the easier new tasks will become, and his/her intellect will grow. For this, you will need a cardboard box big enough for your dog to fit in.

- Begin with your starting phrase.

- Take a cardboard box and place it on its side with the opening facing your dog.

- If your dog shows any interest in the box *click* and reward him/her.

- **Troubleshooting:** If their focus shifts too much in you simply behave interested in the box but do not speak to your dog.

- *Click* and jackpot your dog if they step on the box.

- Once they are going back and forth to the box at rapid speed, start to withhold the click.

- S/he will get frustrated and start offering more behaviors with the box. *Click* and jackpot any progress you like.

- After s/he has been in going in the box consistently and being rewarded for it, tip the box back upright.

- *Click* and reward good intentions.

- Good intentions include; sniffing the opening of the box, looking inside the box, pawing at the box, putting one paw up on the box, putting both paws up on the box, etc.

- Your goal is to have your dog jump inside the box without any guidance or help other than you rewarding the behaviors that you can see will lead to the goal.

Which Hand: This is a game of free shaping that takes a lot of concentration on your dog's part. S/he may even be able to use his/her highly skilled nose! What fun for them!

- Begin by finding the food your dog loves.

- Give your starting phrase and then hide the food in BOTH of your hands. (If your disability prevents you from doing this you can use overturned cups on the ground).

- Present your hands to your dog who should be sitting or standing in front of you.

- Allow your dog to sniff both hands and wait for him/her to paw at one.

- Have a helping do the clicking for you if you use a clicker.

- Once the dog paws at your hand you must *click* and reward him/her by opening your hand to give them the treat.

- Replace the missing food and start again.

- When your dog understands that pawing gets him/her rewarded start to only hide the food in one hand (cup).

- Even if s/he paws at the empty hand, you must open it.

- S/he then realizes that pawing opens the hand but does not directly equal the reward. Instead, s/he must decide which hand has the food and select that hand instead.

- This will come in handy should you need your dog to paw at you to alert you to something in the future. There are a few tasks in the last chapter that you may be able to use this for.

Speak: Now you might be asking, "Why would I teach my dog to speak?" Two reasons, if you can get them to bark on command, you can get them to stop on command, and we will be using this command to bridge a task later in this book. This command may help you with teaching alerts to other noises you may have a hard time hearing such as the doorbell, your phone ringing, someone calling your name, etc. In order to start this command first think about what you can do to make your dog excited enough to bark. Maybe s/he barks when you don't give him/her the food or toy you're withholding or when you get really excited. Whatever works for your dog.

- Be sure to start the lesson with your opening phrase so that your dog understands there is something to learn.

- Present to your dog what you have concluded will work best to get them to speak. (For example, most dogs speak when you increase your energy level).

- As soon as they do bark *click* and reward.

- If you are using a toy to get them to bark, reward them with the toy first and alternate between the toy and reward.

- They should catch on pretty quickly. Once it is clear to you that they understand speaking gets them the reward, add the word "speak" and then do the action that elicits them to bark. *Click* and reward the bark. Due to their thought process of order of events, the word speak will then be associated with the bark.

- Once s/he is doing this consistently, you can withhold the marker to build frustration. Frustration will cause your dog to push harder (in this case, bark more). Mark two barks, then three and so on.

  You've gotten your dog to bark, now how do you get him/her to stop?

Enough: Enough is used to silence your dog once they have alerted you to the noise.

- Begin as you would any lesson.

- Ask him/her to *speak*.

- Allow your dog to bark repeatedly and then firmly say, *enough*.

- As soon as your dog is quiet, *click* and jackpot.

- Timing is very important with this command, and you have to react quickly in order to capture the behavior of your dog ceasing his/her bark.

Hold: Like "speak," hold is another command we are teaching to preface a task. This command will aid in your very first task (see chapter 8).

- Use a stick or toy that your dog enjoys holding.

- We are going to use free shaping with this one so prepare yourself to be patient and hold the toy out in front of you toward your dog.

- Naturally, most dogs will instinctively want to investigate the object. Once they do reward the good intentions.

- Next, they may bump it with their nose, reward them for their pushiness.

- Continue until they are consistently pushing the object with their nose. Then withhold the reward.

- Jackpot any progress such as mouthing.

- Eventually, they will be consistently mouthing the object in order to receive their reward. To build the duration, withhold the reward again. Even if they hold it for a half a second more, jackpot the progress. This is another command that requires a quick response time.

- Once your dog is holding the object start letting go while they steadily hold it.

- You may place one hand under their chin and pet the top of their head with the other hand to encourage the steady grip on the object.

- When you mark and reward once you've gotten to the step of letting go of the object, make sure you go back to holding the object before you release them to give them the reward.

Practice these steps, and we will revisit this command later in the book.

Chapter 6: Neutrality, Desensitization, and Public Preparation Training

Hooray! You're now confident enough in your dog's obedience at home and on walks to bring them out in public. If you have a service vest or special collar for your dog, now is the time to put it on. Reason being, dog's respond well to equipment orientation*. This will put your dog into a perfect state of mind that when the vest is on s/he is at work.

Many places don't allow service dogs in training into their establishment. To better prepare, you can look up the laws in your state. Fortunately, there are a list of stores nationwide that will allow you to bring your service dog in training inside. Do some research for your area as to what stores allow pet dogs, the results may surprise you!

Before you leave the house, exercise your dog! A tired dog will be able to behave more in public which will cause you less stress. Not only will it cause you less stress but your dog will have a more pleasant experience because you won't have to correct them as much. Make sure you pack food rewards/treat pouch, clicker (if applicable), service dog vest, and of course your service dog! One last thing before you load up in the car, give your dog a bathroom break. Use the steps given to you in the previous chapter in order to make this process faster in the future.

When you reach your destination, do not let your dog jump out of the car at will. In fact, I suggest fitting plastic crates in your car if possible. It is safer for your pet in case of a car accident. If you are riding with your dog outside of a crate, however, it will prove beneficial to you during your Public Access Test to practice this manner now. This is why rule number six in chapter three is important to follow. If you never tell your child "no" at home, they will react poorly when you tell them "no" in public. Hopefully, you have yet to bring them out in public before this point. If the last experience they had in public was one in which they felt in charge, you might have to correct them more or take more steps back in the process than if you gave them this new experience with their obedience to fall back on. You can find solace in that the more they learned from you, the more they will look to you for guidance in a new situation. Similar to how you would call your parents in a stressful situation.

After they have calmly gotten out of the car, it is important to get them in the mindset of work. Clip on their service vest and practice some rewarded obedience by your vehicle. Doing this will set the tone for your dog and send a clear message to them as to what is expected from them in this environment. I suggest doing your leash exercise of "follow the leader" before and after your short obedience session. Be sure to jackpot your dog when s/he is fully engaged with you. Once you feel confident with your session, continue inside with your dog walking adjacent to your heel.

I suggest first going to a pet store. Not only are they pet-friendly but if this is your dog's first time out in public s/he will not catch as many glances if s/he behaves badly at all. Many of the pets that enter these stores have little to no training, so people are used to unruly dogs. Of course, your dog won't be unruly because you've followed these rules and steps consistently. In fact, I reckon you get a few compliments. Remember no one should pet or feed your dog with his/her vest on. If you want to allow this behavior, the vest should come off first. However, for the first month or so I would not allow this whatsoever. If someone tries to grab your dog's attention, think back to your training. Say your dog's name and as soon as s/he makes eye contact with you, jackpot! What a great milestone! Keep the store visit short and sweet. Don't ask for too much from them, the goal of this trip is simply exposure and general good behavior. Any obedience you do ask from your dog on the first trip should be rewarded. Use every person that walks by as a teaching moment. When a person or group of people walk by, note how your dog reacts. S/he is not allowed to sniff other people (or merchandise for that matter) as they walk by. End a good note! Your second trip should be in the same store (even the same day but after a well-deserved break). This time, only reward moments that impress you. For instance, if your dog has been laying down on command every time but slower than you'd like, jackpot him/her when s/he lays down faster. It may not be the speed you'd like yet, but it's a step closer to your goal. This is the difference between practice and application. We have been practicing for about a month at this point, now it's time to apply what you've taught your dog.

The second store I would suggest going to is any home improvement store. Now that you trust your dog will behave in public, it's time to expose them to minor stressors. These stressors could be loud carts, saws, public announcement speakers, crowded aisles, etc. Start small, walk past someone with a cart. If your dog behaves well and ignores the stimulus, *click* and reward. Jackpot when s/he ignores a larger stressor. What about when s/he reacts badly to stimulus? Ignore your dog if s/he seems stressed. If you coddle their fear, you will validate their reaction. It's the same reason dogs are afraid of lightning. S/he shows slight concern, and someone comforts them, although, with good intentions, the dog will further believe s/he is correct in his/her fear.

If you do find something your dog is unsure about, do some of your obedience session at a distance your dog feels comfortable at – probably away from the stressor. Slowly get closer to the stressor while practicing your obedience. Dogs are terrible at multitasking. If they are focused on you and their obedience as they come closer to the stressor, then soon they will behave normally even when they are closed to the stressor. They will realize nothing bad happens.

Imagine you're in a new school and everything is new and scary. However, in your old school, you were a math wiz, and that's where you felt most comfortable. All of your classes in this new school would be hard to adjust to until you went in to math class. Once class starts you're in your zone and all other issues and stressors of the day melt away at that moment. When your dog is confident with their obedience, it becomes their comfort zone in new environments until they have been in so many new environments that they feel confident to tackle any new situation.

Another environment that your dog needs to get used to is the veterinarian's office. It's imperative that your dog does not associate the vets with negative memories. In order to do this, you must take time out to bring your dog to your regular vet just to visit the staff and have them give him/her treats. If s/he only goes to the vet to get shots s/he will start to develop a negative association with the office. However, thanks to your pup's understanding of probability, s/he will take the risk in order to receive the reward if they more so often get the reward.

The more places you bring your dog, the more comfortable your dog will be in any given situation. The more new things you teach them, the better they will become at learning. If you don't have stairs in your home, I will practice walking up and down stairs with your dog. If you're in a wheelchair work on safely loading and unloading elevators. If you are asked about your service dog be sure to be calm and educational on the general need for service dogs.

Crossing the street should be easy. Of course, follow your mother's rule of stopping at the curb and looking both ways before you cross. Prepare to pop the leash if your dog forges ahead. S/he should stop on a dime when you stop. If you do have to correct him/her, practice walking up to the curb a few times and preemptively pop the leash simultaneously when you stop. Go back to the rule of three old one new. For three repetitions, walk up to the curb and pop at the same time. Do not give any commands, praise or treats. If you pop the leash and treat you will not be giving your dog a clear picture of what you want. On the fourth repetition, don't pop the leash right away. If your dog stops on time, *click* and jackpot. Alternatively, if s/he does not stop on time, pop the leash a little more firmly and do *not* reward. Continue until you succeed. If you were to correct your dog and then reward them for getting back into position in the same repetition, they would continue to do the incorrect behavior to take the correction to receive the reward anyway. Especially if the risk is worth the reward.

Practice down-stays at the end of the aisle as people walk by, you may tell your dog "good" but try to say it only when a person passes. The real test will be when a dog or person walks by. If someone stops to try to engage with them (including dogs) calmly and politely explain that your pup is in training. First, just reward and release them after one passing person. Jackpot for children or dogs passing. Walk to another aisle and repeat. Another impressive pass your dog should be rewarded greatly for is when a shopping cart passes closely while s/he is in a down-stay.

The third place you should go (weather permitting) is a restaurant with an outdoor eating area. During the Public Access Test, at least one time your dog will be tested with food on the ground. It is important to your dog's health and general manners that s/he never eats food off of the ground. When you sit down at your table, your dog should be out of the way of the customers and staff. Ask your dog to lay down underneath the table by your feet. I would suggest trying this first at home.

- Your dog is in a down-stay.

- Be sure you have a firm grasp on the leash, it should be loose, but you should be ready to correct him/her

- Drop food about 4 feet from your dog.

- If s/he lunges, pop the leash (reaction time is important). If s/he accidentally eats the food, it's okay. Just re-adjust your timing and distance.

- If your dog does not go for the dropped food, pick the food back up and then *click* and jackpot your pup.

- They should remain in a down-stay.

- This is a great example of when you should use the three old fourth new repetitions.

- Build duration from the time the food hits the ground to when you pick it up and reward him/her.

You've spent all your time with your dog over the weeks you've been training. But sometimes you'll need to hand the leash to someone you're with while you go out of sight. This is tested during the Public Access Test. Your dog must remain calm and wait for your return without showing stress. At home, practice this first with the crate. Randomly, 15-20 times a day put your dog in the crate and shut the door for 1-5 minutes at a time for no reason. For the first day, have the crate in an area where s/he can see you while s/he is in it. Then, move the crate to a more secluded area. Once s/he is consistently calm, have a helper hold the leash while you leave out of sight briefly and come back. Do not say goodbye or hello to your dog. The excitement of you coming back will build separation anxiety because they are anticipating your return. Instead, when you come back to your dog, neutrally take the leash from your helper, walk a few feet and *click* and reward your dog. Ignore any separation anxiety. Correcting it will be giving them attention which is what is causing the anxiety. Once s/he has been rewarded a few times for not showing anxious behavior, wean them off the rewarding.

In order to desensitize your dog to grooming it is a good idea that you do it regularly. Regardless of your training, your dog should always look good in the public eye. This desensitization will not only help you at the vet's office but also during the Canine Good Citizen Test if you choose to take it. Frequently probe your dog's mouth, ears, and paws in preparation and reward them at the end of every session.

Chapter 7: Tasks

Finally! You're ready to learn the tasks that will give you a new quality of life and further build your relationship with your dog. Throughout this chapter, you may pick what is appropriate to you and your lifestyle and apply it to your dog's training.

Bring: This task may be used for a variety of reasons. Many times you will drop an item you may not be able to pick up or perhaps something is out of reach, and you need your service dog to retrieve it for you. You'll notice this task stems off of the command to "hold."

- We left off at "hold" where your dog will willingly hold an item for your decided amount of time.

- We will now add the action of picking up the item. Find a short table, chair, or box that is about chest height on your dog.

- Rest the item your dog is most comfortable picking up on the surface.

- While close to your dog (the same distance you've been practicing at) point to the object and encourage the dog to pick up the item.

- Once they do, take hold of the item from their mouth (they should continue to hold) and *click* and reward your dog.

- **Troubleshooting:** Just as we did when your dog got out of position from a sit or down, if your dog lets of the object, they should be ignored until they re-grip it.

- Continue these steps until you have consistency. When it is consistent, add the word "bring" to your hand gestures (pointing).

- Once proficient, start to move (you and your dog) further away from the surface and object. Start at about a foot away.

- Gradually create more and more distance and jackpot progression.

- Once you have a good amount of distance lower the treat to a surface that meets your dog's front ankles.

- When you lower the object, you should go back to the first distance you started at. Again, build distance for this new height.

- Eventually, once you are confident have the item on the ground. Jackpot your dog for the progression of picking it up and then build distance and consistency.

- Try now sitting in a chair and dropping the item at your feet. Ask your dog to "bring" the item and reward the jackpot.

- **Troubleshooting:** If you struggle at any point during these steps, retrace your progress to the last step s/he was proficient at and slowly build off of that.

- Now it's time to start creating a better generalization with the command. If you were using a stick, switch to another object you think s/he may enjoy holding. The more objects you do these steps with, the more neutral the command will become and s/he will pick up any item. You can even start giving the items names! Remember, when you introduce something new, you supplement it with something old. With this new object it's important, you start by holding it first as we did in the obedience chapter. Don't worry, your dog has done this before and will quickly catch in and progress through the steps much faster.

Hearing Aid: Dogs can be trained to alert us to many noises. These include alarms, phone's ringing, someone calling your name, a knock at the door or even a car behind us! However, for this task, we will simply be teaching your dog to alert us to a text message. If this does not apply to your life but you still would like for your dog to alert you to another noise, simply apply these steps to the noise of your choosing.

- First, get your phone and through the settings app, find notifications and select the notification sound that you use for your text messaging. It should play each time you press it.

- Remember how we taught your dog how to speak on command? Great! We will be using that as well.

- Give your lesson starting phrase and gain your dog's attention.

- Press the noise on your phone and then immediately ask your dog to speak afterward.

- Reward your dog for doing so. Ultimately this is giving speak a nickname. Your dog will know that when the noise plays, you tell him/her to speak. Eventually, they will cut you to the chase and speak as soon as they hear the sound because they want to get the reward as soon as possible.

- You should continue these sessions until you no longer have to tell your dog to speak after the noise.

- Once s/he is being consistent, try applying it outside of the sessions. If your dog seems curious towards the noise but stuck or confused, it is okay to help him/her put by prompting them to bark with your "speak" command.

- Now the fun part! Once your dog is understanding both bring [insert item here] and how to alert to your phone's text message notification, you can have your phone go off from across the room (or even in another room) and ask your dog to retrieve it for you!

Open: Depending on your disability, you may find it difficult to open and close doors. In this step by step, I will teach you the basics of how to teach your dog to open cabinet doors.

- Choose a cabinet door that is easily accessible to your dog.

- Take out a rope or scarf and entice your dog to play tug.

- As soon as s/he tugs on it just once, *click* and reward.

- Add the word open now if you'd like and make sure s/he is tugging just once.

- Next, tie the rope or scarf to the cabinet's knob or handle.

- Use your hand to entice the dog to bite and give you command to open.

- Jackpot the progress.

Close: Now the cabinet door is open, and it must be shut. Do you remember the game where we taught your dog to touch your hand with his nose? Great! We will be applying it to this task!

- Have a sticky note or piece of solid colored tape attached to your palm, give your dog the touch command and reward them for nudging the tape.

- Once s/he is consistent, move the tape to the cabinet where the dog should push on it in order to close it.

- Tell your dog to touch and be patient. *Click* and jackpot if s/he even sniffs the cabinet.

- **Troubleshooting:** If your dog is having difficulties making the connection, do as we did for "touch" which is to hide food underneath. In this case, hide a piece of food underneath the tape so s/he can smell it but they are unable to eat it. *Click* and jackpot any interest in it.

- Once your dog is offering this command (trust me they will, it is fun and easy for them!) Add the word "close" just before they are predicted to push the tape on the cabinet.

- Once s/he is proficiently pushing the tape, make the tape about half the size. Continue for a few consistent reps. Make sure you jackpot the progress.

- Soon you will be able to take the tape away and give the command to close, and your dog will push the cabinet door shut.

- This is when you will add distance. Which means... can you guess?

- That's right! ADD THE TAPE BACK. Bring on something new, add some old.

Grounding (Deep Pressure Therapy): Many people who suffer from anxiety and panic attack may benefit from using grounding techniques. Often times this focuses on your senses – sight, smell, hearing, taste, and touch. However, many benefit from pressure being applied on top of them. Most people use a weighted blanket but lucky for you, you have a living breathing furry weighted blanket who loves you. In order to teach this task, you must be laying down or sitting. I suggest first sitting and then progressing to laying down.

- Begin by sitting in a chair with your dog beside you or in front of you (whichever will serve your dog as the easiest way to access your lap).

- Pat your lap and encourage your dog to jump up on to your lap so that his/her chest and legs are resting on you.

- *Click* and reward your dog.

- Once s/he is proficiently jumping on your lap, lure his/her head down so that his/her chin is on your lap or stomach. *Click* and jackpot in position.

- Begin to add the name and slowly take away the lure.

- Hold the treats opposite of your dog at your side and allow them to come to the (as opposed to you luring them there) so that they land in the correct position with their chin on your lap.

- Next, we will move onto this task in the laying down position.

- Your dog should make the connection, however, if s/he does not, consider practicing in a recliner first.

- This time we will pat our chest and encourage the dog to lay heavily there. The pressure should be soothing, and your dog should be calm.

- Once you have your dog laying with his chin and chest on your torso on command, it is time to begin building duration.

- Hold the treat opposite of your dog's starting position and give your command. Withhold your marker for one Mississippi and then *click* and reward.

- Continue to build duration and then become consistently inconsistent. This means the way and order in which you practice your repetitions will stay the same while the timing will vary randomly.

- The nice thing about this is that the cues you give off during a panic attack will prompt your dog to "ground you" if you are consistent about asking every time. You can even fake panic attacks by showing some of the symptoms such as shaking or hyperventilating in order to practice your repetitions.

Undressing: Many people are incapable of efficiently undressing themselves. Inflexibility and other injuries or disabilities may result in the inability to independently take off your jacket, pants, shirt, and socks to name a few articles. In this step by step guide, we will be teaching your dog how to remove your sock and jacket! There are similarities between this and the task "open." First, let's remove your socks, I hope you aren't ticklish!

- Begin by sitting in a chair with your dog in front of you. Holding a sock entice him/her to tug on it. This should be easy for your dog since he had seen this pictures before when he learned how to open the cabinet for you.

- There is no need to jackpot this behavior.

- Move the sock between your legs (if you are able to, hold it between your knees or calves, if not holding it in position with your hand is acceptable) continue you as long as your dog is progressing steadily and without flaw.

- Place the socks on your feet so that they are already half off and ask your dog to "pull off your socks" if s/he gets stuck backtrack and add the command at the last point of proficiency. Reward good intentions.

- When s/he finally does remove your socks from your foot, *click* jackpot!

- Incrementally start over with your sock further and further on your foot until it is completely on. Then ask your dog to remove your socks(s).

- **Troubleshooting:** Note that it may be strange for your dog to grab your sock and have to be careful not to bite your toes. If s/he seems hesitant, slowly give your dog more sock to work with until s/he is comfortable then slowly move it back down.

- **Jacket!** By now, you have taken off your sock, and now it is time for your jacket to come off. Before it can come off, however, you must first unzip it. Correction, your dog must unzip it.

- Tie a piece of string or shoelace to your zipper. It should hang about six to eight inches from the zipper.

- Start with the zipper only a few notches up from the bottom.

- Entice your dog to pull the string. Once s/he does, *click* and reward the good intentions. Even if he doesn't pull it all the way open.

- Once he is consistently pulling the zipper open, move the zipper up half way and cut the string in half to three to four inches.

- Only move forward if s/he has successfully and consistently been opening the zipper completely. Add the word "zipper" or "pull zipper" at this time.

- Next, keep the zipper at the halfway point and cut the string smaller, so it's just a little tag hanging off of the zipper tab.

- Ask your dog to *pull the zipper* and jackpot the progression.

- Add the string back on after your dog has mastered the small amount of string at the halfway point. Move the zipper all the way to the top.

- Your dog is allowed to jump up on to your lap in order to successfully pull the zipper tab. Reward pulling even if not 100% successful in opening the zipper completely.

- Once s/he is comfortable with doing this and is consistently pulling the zipper all the way open, you may return the string back to a small tag.

- After s/he is proficient in pulling the small tag, remove the string completely and start at the bottom again.

- **Troubleshooting:** If s/he is having trouble, attach the string for three consistent repetitions at the bottom of the zipper and for the fourth repetition without the string. Repeat until successful. Jackpot the progress and end on a good note!

- Now that your zipper is open, it is time to you remove the jacket as well.

- Grab the sleeve of your jacket and encourage your pup to pull the wrist. Reward this behavior and give it a command such as "undress."

- Continue once proficient, by slipping only one arm inside the sleeve going from a bit past your fingertips and ending at your elbow.

- Ask your dog to "undress" you and encourage him/her to grab and pull your sleeve just as you did before it was on your arm. *Click* and reward.

- Then, slide the sleeve further up your arm so that the opening of the sleeve is around your wrist but the jacket sleeve should still end at your elbow.

- After your dog has mastered this, put the whole sleeve on so the shoulder of the jacket is resting on your shoulder. This should be an easy transition for your dog.

- Next one sleeve and two shoulders. Not much difficulty here visually for your dog. However, it may be physically more difficult for him/her to get it passed your shoulders. Depending on your capabilities, you may help your dog by maneuvering your shoulders to make this easier as he pulls on your sleeve.

- The real difficulty comes when you put your other sleeve on as well. If you can maneuver your arm so that the first sleeve is easy to come off and then encourage your dog to try the other sleeve. This may be weird for some dogs because of their poor proprioception. Practice makes perfect!

- Make sure to jackpot any impressive progress and end on a good note! All sessions should only be ten to fifteen minutes long. Especially for the complex tasks such as this.

Depositing Items in a Receptacle: Now that you have taught your dog to undress you and carry items, you can teach them how to bring your laundry to a laundry basket and drop them inside of it.

- First, get your laundry basket. Give your starting phrase and then put it in between you and your dog.

- Use an item that your dog is comfortable holding with, and set your dog up about a foot from the basket.

- Have your dog hold the item and walk him/her forward until their head is above the opening of the basket.

- As soon as his/her head is above the basket give the command, you would like to use such as "basket" and then *click* and reward. This time, however (unlike you have done in the past) you will not hold the item before you click. Instead, you will let the item fall into the basket.

- Do this a few times until s/he is dropping the item when you say "basket" and *click* the action of dropping the item into the basket.

- Next, give the command earlier. Give the command directly before you start walking. This step may be confusing for your dog, but allow him/her to make mistakes. It may take a moment for him/her to realize and understand that the basket plays a key role in the task. At first, your dog may think "basket" is a command to simply drop whatever is in their mouth.

- **Troubleshooting:** Let him/her get it wrong a few times without being rewarded, set the basket up closer and then walk him/her to the basket without giving the command. Wait to see if s/he drops the item in the basket silently while your dog hovers his/her head over the opening. *Click* and jackpot if s/he does so.

- **Troubleshooting:** Set the basket up about a foot from your dog and give the command right before his/her head is above the opening of the basket. Only reward him/her for getting it inside the basket.

- Once proficient with two feet and giving the command before the walk to the basket, start having your dog walk to the basket on his/her own.

- Hold the leash, hand the dog the item you have been using and ask them to "basket." If you have done the previous steps proficiently, s/he should drop the item in the basket. If s/he does not, please retrace your steps of progression back to where s/he was best and take it slower this time.

- After completing this to a point of 100% consistent accuracy, you may continue to incrementally add distance between you and the basket. The difference between this step and the ones prior is that you will be stationary and your dog will be leaving you to go to the basket. Use your leash to guide him/her.

- Eventually, s/he will be doing this quickly and excitedly and running back to you for his/her reward. Make sure you are giving the command, letting your dog bring the item to the basket, dropping the item in the basket and clicking only when s/he drops the item in the basket.

- **Troubleshooting:** However, if your dog has been having trouble leaving you to go to the basket, click and reward good intentions but only jackpot when s/he makes it into the basket. Play with the distance to make it easier and to better set your dog up for jackpot opportunities.

- Have fun with this task and start training with the same steps for throwing trash away or even recycling!

Clear Room/House: Many people suffering from Post-Traumatic Stress Disorder or other forms of stress-induced anxiety have a need to feel completely safe and secure. Often times they will have a fear that when they enter a room or house that there could be a potential threat inside especially if the room or house is dark. Two things a service dog can do in order to provide a feeling of comfort to their human in this situation is check the room or house and turn on lights. First, we will teach your dog how to clear a room.

- Start with a small well lit room.

- Give your starting phrase and bring your dog around the perimeter of the room. Click and reward the dog every time he/she is following along the wall's surface. Even if it is just a few steps.

- Eventually, your dog will catch on that s/he gets paid for following the perimeter of the room, and you can start building duration until you are only jackpot-ing at the end or completion of the room.

- Keep these sessions short and only allow the dog in this room when you are training the task.

- Moving forward, hook your dog to a long line and slowly move yourself away from the wall, allowing the dog to stay on the wall. The first time you move away and your dog stays, you should jackpot him/her.

- Once you are standing in the middle of the room and your dog is consistently scanning the perimeter without you moving or guiding him/her, you can start to move incrementally towards the door.

- Make sure you are casting your dog towards the wall each time by pointing and giving the command.

- Once you are by the door and able to cast your dog around the perimeter and back to you, you may try stepping outside of the room and casting him/her inside. If s/he has any trouble understanding what you are asking, go back to the step s/he was most proficient at.

- After this, go back inside and ask your dog to scan the perimeter while the lights are off. If s/he is successful, move outside of the room and casting into the dark room.

- **Troubleshooting:** If your dog is afraid to enter the dark room, try three repetitions with you inside the dark room and one with the lights on at the beginning of the search (with you outside the room) and when s/he is about halfway through the scan, turn off the lights. Alternatively, you can cast into the dark room and walk him/her on the leash into the dark room and lead him/her around the perimeter. Jackpot only when s/he searches completely in the dark.

- Jackpot any major progression and always end on a good note! Make sure to close with your concluding phrase.

- Next, to clear an entire house, we want to again start from inside. Begin with the room you had been using to train the room clearance.

- *Click* and reward your dog a small amount and then cast him/her into another (well lit) room. If s/he seems confused, guide him/her around the perimeter and jackpot the end of the room just as you did the first room.

- This doesn't have to be a room with a door. It could also be an area of the house such as the kitchen or living room. The idea is to do it for all the rooms until you can cast from a main room and your dog will search the perimeter of each room in the house. Eventually, you will be outside of your house (following the same steps as the room clearance task) the more rooms and houses you do the more the dog will generalize houses and rooms and better understand what you are asking. This will build neutrality in all environments for this task.

Light Switches On and Off: Now that your dog can search an entire house (or at least a room) it would be nice if s/he could turn on the lights to ease your anxiety further. This is also useful in the mornings when you are getting out of bed and when you are going to bed at night. The easiest thing you can do is purchase a touch activate lamp for your home. We will first go over how to train for the touch activated lamp and then move on to the more complex task of light switches.

- Begin with your starting phrase.

- Have the light plugged in and in front of you and your dog.

- If you have taught the close command for cabinets, this should be easy.

- Get a piece of tape or sticky note and place it on the lamp where the dog should be touching.

- Ask your dog to "touch" (with his/her nose only, I will explain later).

- **Troubleshooting:** If your dog is having a hard time understanding what is expected of him/her then go back to basics. Stick the piece of tape to your hand and start moving your hand towards the lamp so your dog is used to where his/her neck should stretch or bend to.

- After your dog has been sufficiently pressing the tape on the lamp, add distance. Start from a foot away and only build distance if s/he is consistent with the previous distance.

- Once you are happy with the distance, go back to the lamp and do three repetitions with the tape at a short distance and then cut the tape in half and do a fourth. Begin adding the word you would like to use such as "lamp" or "light." Continue until your dog is proficient with the smaller piece of tape. Add distance.

- Content with your distance and successful repetitions move back to the lamp. Take the tape completely off. And give your command. If s/he is confused, add the tape back for three repetitions and for the fourth one take the tape off. Continue until your goal is reached and add distance the same as you did in previous steps.

- Now that s/he is proficient with the touch lamp it is time to master light switches. You will need to get a little creative and crafty with your tape for this one. Although not conventional, this is the fastest way I have found to communicate this task to a dog.

- Begin with a piece of tape on the wall about eye level with your dog.

- Ask your dog to "touch" it with his/her nose only. Then, eventually, we will be asking your dog to put his/her paws up on the wall in order to switch on and off the light. It is not only more complicated to maneuver for the dog, but it could also damage the wall if s/he used his/her paw to hit the light switch. Especially at the beginning when s/he is just getting the hang of it.

- Start moving the tape higher and higher up in small increments. If you do this too quickly, your dog may not feel confident enough to try to reach it.

- Move it up until the tape is at the same height as the light switches. This should be around four feet high.

- Do a few sessions just getting your dog comfortable with reaching this height.

- Next, (here is where your crafting abilities will be put to the test) fashion a light switch out if the tape. I used a flat piece of tape on the wall with another piece of tape folded in half the long way. At the ends of the tape, I would flare them out in order to stick it to the tape on the wall. This should be placed at your dog's eye-level.

- Ask your dog to touch and reward good intentions. The goal is for them to push up on the flap. Add your command for this now.

- The first time s/he pushes up on the flap, *click* and jackpot. Only jackpot the pushes up and then only reward the pushes up. Use your judgment with your dog on when you should make the switch to only rewarding flipping the flap up.

- Build distance with the makeshift light switch at this height. Reward good intentions.

- Slowly move the makeshift tape light switch to the height of the real light switch.

- Once your dog is comfortable with this height, add distance. Make sure you are clicking and rewarding good intentions whenever you add more distance or height. However, you should only move forward if they are consistently pushing up on the flap with their nose.

- Now that your dog is a pro with the tape switch fold a piece of tape over the switch and secure it in place around the actual switch lever with another piece of tape if necessary.

- Start close to the switch and give your dog the command you've been using for the tape made light switch. If s/he has trouble with this go back to the last step s/he was confident with.

- Reward good intentions such as jumping up, jumping up and sniffing the light switch, or jumping up and nudging the switch. These will all lead to your goal.

- Jackpot any time s/he makes progress and end on a good note!

- Once your dog is successfully turning on the light you can then start leaving the light on and ask him/her to hit the light, s/he should get frustrated and try other ways to touch the switch. Accidentally s/he will eventually turn off the light, and this should be jackpot-ed. This requires a lot of patience.

- By the time s/he understands that the switch can be both turned on and off, you may add a different word to differentiate between the two actions. Depending on the dog you may need to add a separate command or your dog may understand if the switch is up to flip it down and vice versa.

Pulling Blanket Off: Many people with service dogs can suffer from depression, and like many people with depression, sometimes it's difficult to get out of bed. Having the responsibility of a dog may sometimes be enough incentive. However, in some cases you may need a little extra. In other instances, you may be physically unable to remove the blanket from your body. This is a fun and easy task for your dog, especially if they understand some of the previous commands such as undress, open, and zipper.

- As I've mentioned before, every dog is different and thus what works for some dogs may not work for others.

- With that being said, your dog, for instance, may not want to clamp down on your blanket. However, if you are creative, you can tie a piece of rope to the corner of your blanket first and proceed from there. For the purposes of explaining, your dog will be pulling the blanket (if you need help with the rope transition apply the zipper foundation in the section labeled "undressing").

- Start the session with your starting phrase and sit down in a chair with a blanket over your lap.

- Entice your dog to tug on the blanket (or rope if you so choose to use one).

- S/he has seen this before if you have done the other tasks so s/he should catch in fairly quick.

- Next, lay down on the bed with the blanket over you. Entice your pup to pull the blanket. Reward good intentions and jackpot them if they pull it off completely.

- **Bonus Tip:** If you want to get fancy, you can make the command your alarm clock so that when your alarm goes off your dog rips the blanket off of you!

Post: Many people who require a service dog appreciate space (even people without the need for a service dog). Some even require it if they suffer from anxiety or another psychological disorder. Dogs can mitigate this anxiety by serving as a barrier between you and other people. This comes in handy in lines and/or in crowded areas. To start this lesson grab a towel like the one you used when you taught your dog the place command.

- Put the towel on the ground and hook your dog to a leash.

- Lure your dog to the towel with the leash and reward him/her for standing on it.

- Once your dog catches on to why s/he is being rewarded, ask your dog to sit or lay down when on the towel. For the purposes of explaining we will ask your dog to down.

- Once s/he is proficiently moving to the towel and laying down without being asked to lay down, give the name "post" and lead your dog to the towel. *Click* and jackpot. You may use whichever command you like best for this task.

- Next, stand in front of the towel and give your dog the task command you choose. Help him/her by using the leash to guide him/her behind you. Jackpot.

- Then add the "down" command. Try three repetitions with telling him/her to down and the fourth time without it. Jackpot the progression.

- Now it's time to take the leash away. Try it without the leash. If s/he is confused, use food to lure him/her onto the towel behind you. Reward for getting into position behind you, not for laying down.

- Once s/he is used to going behind you without the aid of the leash, then add the "down" command again.

- The last step is taking away the towel.

- **Troubleshooting:** If your dog is confused by the absence of the towel, fold the towel, so it is smaller and do three consistently successful repetitions and for the fourth repetition, take the towel away. Repeat this until s/he has a successful repetition without the towel, *click,* jackpot, and end on that good note!

- Another form of post is standing in front of you in order to create a barrier. This doesn't have to be a command. Many people who utilize this behavior are triggered by people walking up to them too quickly. You can use this as a cue for your dog to step in front of you when you are stationary (so you don't trip over them). The cue is a person walking too quickly towards you.

- First, you must teach the same action as post at your back. This means bringing the towel to your front side and luring your dog with a leash to your front. Step by step remove your training wheels to the point where your dog will follow the guide of your leash to your front on the towel.

- Grab your best-trusted helper and set them up about 10 feet away from you. The distance is really up to you.

- Have them walk towards you at a pace that would upset you if they were a stranger or someone you didn't know as well. Make sure your dog is looking forward.

- Once they get about halfway, guide your dog in front of you. *Click* and Jackpot!

- This will most likely take many reps. Keep the lessons short, and once s/he is preemptively moving in front of you by picking up on the cue and putting the picture together, you can take away the towel. Jackpot the progress or any repetition that impressed you.

Crowd Control: Service dogs can help people who do not do well in crowded areas. In the previous task we talked about what your dog should do if you are stationary, but what about if you're walking? You still want people to keep their distance as to not crowd you. The behavior of circling around you is an effective task that will serve you as your own personal crowd control.

- Begin standing in one spot, stationary.

- Have your dog on leash and guide him from your side around your body and back to the same side. *Click* and reward.

- It is important you choose one side and one direction for the circling to give your dog the best chance at understanding what is asked of him/her.

- Give the command once your dog is effortlessly guided around you by the leash.

- When you give the command make sure you are giving the command *and then* guiding him/her around your body. This will make the process for your dog easier, and s/he will listen to your verbal commands rather than what your body is doing. If you do the action of guiding your dog during or before the command, your dog will be looking for the gesture of you guiding him instead of the verbal command.

- Once s/he is beating you to the leash guidance, you can add more circles. Start with one and only reward (Jackpot the first time) when the dog goes around twice.

- Eventually, your dog will understand s/he must go around more than once in order to receive the reward. Waiting your dog out at this point will encourage him or her to keep circling. Frustration will build his/her drive to continue circling around you until you click and reward.

- Alternatively, you can continue to add circles incrementally (only moving forward once your dog is proficient with the last number of circles).

- I suggest getting up to seven to ten continuous circles and then begin marking at random. The randomness will make your dog continue to circle you just keeping an ear out for the marker as a cue to stop and get paid (rewarded)

- Once this is easy for you, take one step while your dog is circling and then *click* and jackpot.

- **Troubleshooting:** If your dog stops when you take a step, reward him three times for circling while you're stationary and on the fourth repetition, just slightly move your leg forward as if you were going to take a step. *Click* and reward. Move on from this incrementally and Jackpot the first step.

- Then take two steps and jackpot. Keep these sessions short and fun! Continue until you can walk in a straight line and your dog continuously circles you.

- To start turns, begin stationary and simply turn your body 90 degrees in one direction, *click* and jackpot your dog. Then you can start adding the turning after steps forward. Soon you will be walking fluidly with your dog creating a buffer zone between you and the world.

- Remember, any time your dog gets confused go back to the last step s/he was confident with.

Pulling a Wheelchair up a Ramp: Many people with mobility issues have difficulty walking up and down stairs. If you have this issue, you may be able to use your service dog to stabilize yourself when going up and down the stairs. However, for those people who are wheelchair bound, they must use a ramp. Depending on their physical condition, they may not be able to physically wheel their chair up the ramp. For this, we can utilize your service dog. Please make sure your dog is in good health and strong enough to pull your body weight plus the chair. If you are wheelchair bound, to start, you may need to sit in a chair or on the floor at the beginning. You should also find a rope that you can later safely attach to your wheelchair.

- Begin with your starting phrase.

- Present the rope to your dog and entice him/her to pull on it. Reward any pulling and jackpot methodical straight back pulls.

- Allow him/her to pull your torso forward in a straight line and jackpot this calm behavior. Ignore thrashing and do not reward until the dog is calm.

- S/he should be consistently pulling while walking backward until s/he hears the marker and is rewarded.

- When you feel confident that your dog understands this, find an object (such as a plastic laundry basket) you can attach the rope to.

- With the rope attached, entice your dog to pull the rope again. *Click* and jackpot any pulling that moves the object. Reward steady steps back. You may add your command word here.

- Next, add more weight (easy if you are using a plastic laundry basket).

- If your dog does well with this, take the weight off/out again and go to your ramp.

- If possible, lower your ramp, so it is at less of an incline.

- Place the object your dog will be pulling towards the top with the rope facing closest to the top.

- *Click* and reward your dog for pulling on the rope at all but only jackpot when s/he pulls the basket to the top.

- Move the basket lower on the ramp at the same incline. Continue until s/he is proficient.

- Once s/he is successfully pulling the basket in a methodical manner all the way from the bottom of the ramp to the top at the lowest incline, move the ramp up higher and start over. Then start adding the weight back.

- When you add the weight back, decline the ramp again and start the. Basket at the top.

- When your dog is confident with this start to only reward him/her for pulling the basket from the bottom to a foot past the ramp at the top.

- The reason we are taking such small baby steps is that we want to ensure the safety of not only you but also of your dog. The more comfortable your dog is with this task, the safer you will be.

- Next, go back to a flat surface and safely attach the rope you have been using to your empty wheelchair.

- Present the rope attached to your empty wheelchair to your dog and ask him/her to pull it.

- Jackpot when the wheelchair moves. Reward good intentions.

- When s/he is consistently moving the wheelchair in a methodical manner by pulling it and backing up straight, you may bring them to the ramp. Remember, they should only let go of the rope and stop pulling when they hear their marker.

- At the ramp, set it at a lower angle and place the wheelchair at the bottom. Try three repetitions of pulling the empty wheelchair on the flat ground and then position it appropriately at the bottom of the ramp.

- Set your dog up at the bottom and give your dog the command to pull the wheelchair. Reward any pulling but Jackpot if they pull it all the way to the top. Make sure to encourage them the whole time as this may not be easy for them.

- Slowly raise the incline of the ramp and begin only rewarding for when they pull the wheelchair a foot past the ramp at the top.

- When they are consistently pulling the empty wheelchair at all the way to a foot past the top at the highest incline, you can start adding weights to the wheelchair. I suggest using books or gym style weights if you have them.

- Not quite there yet! Put about half your body weight worth of weights in the wheelchair and have him/her drag it on a flat surface. Only reward when s/he is calm and holding the rope. S/he should only let go when s/he hears the marker.

- Next, add the rest of the weight. In fact, it doesn't hurt to add a few more pounds than what you weigh. Continue for the new weight on a flat surface.

- Make sure he is doing this to proficiency one hundred percent of the time before you move to the ramp.

- Once at the ramp, again move the incline to a low level. Take half the weight out and have him/her pull the wheelchair with half your body weight up the ramp. Jackpot for completion, reward attempts and always encourage while s/he is pulling.

- Slowly raise the incline with half the weight in it.

- When s/he is proficient at that weight, move to full weight and lower the ramp again. Thank you for being so patient, but you will understand why if you either skip head or witness your dog dropping the fully weighted wheelchair down the ramp!

- Again, only jackpot your dog for pulling the weighted wheelchair fully up the ramp a foot past the edge. Only reward a calm straight line.

- Once your dog is pulling the fully weighted wheelchair all the way up a full incline consistently and safely every time, it is time to put you in the hot seat!

- Of course, you will first do this on a flat surface. Have your dog first pull the faux weighted wheelchair on a flat surface about three consistent repetitions and then on the fourth repetition replace the weights with yourself.

- ONLY reward your dog if s/he is not letting go and pulling until they hear the marker. Do not move forward until this is accurate.

- Only *click* when they are a foot past the top of the ramp. When you feel confident in your dog begin raising the ramp. If you start to feel less confident practice a lower incline until you are ready to move up again.

- I suggest at least fifty clean repetitions of each incremental incline before you try the ramp at full height. Safety first!

- Remember to keep it fun and encouraging for your dog!

Medication Reminders: Many of us can be forgetful as the hours tick day by day. For some, missing the time they need to take their medication could be detrimental to their health and lives. Even if you set an alarm, you may be hard of hearing or be away from the alarm at the time. This is where your dog comes in. Ever notice how your dog knows exactly when dinner time is? This is because they are experts at routine. They love routine! That being said, it is only natural to utilize their internal clock for the purposes of keeping you healthy. There are a few ways we can do this and a few alerts as well. For the purposes of explaining we will be teaching your dog how to find your medication and bring it to you at the time of day, you take it every day. This may take a while for your dog to learn. I find the best way is to focus on this task for the majority of the lessons you do. First, we must teach your dog what your medications are, where they are kept, and how to retrieve them.

- Start off the lesson with your starting phrase.

- I suggest keeping your medication container(s) in a plastic ziplock bag for the safety of your dog.

- Start with an empty plastic bag and repeat the steps for hold and bring. Create distance. Once s/he is proficiently bringing the plastic bag to you, add the medication inside the plastic zip lock bag.

- Then start to add your medication alarm sound (this alarm sound should be unique to your medication). Use the alarm sound immediately followed by the command. Only jackpot when s/he reacts to the alarm sound and not your voice command.

- Once s/he is doing this consistently you can place the medication in the location it usually is.

- Start close by the location and play the alarm sound followed by your voice command.

- Slowly add distance every time s/he is doing well.

- Start playing the sound from other rooms. If s/he gets confused go to your previous successful step.

- When your dog's doing this without flaw and having fun. Stop doing the lessons. That's right! This fun game ends and becomes a daily treat (this may not happen quickly).

- Let's say you take your medication at 9 A.M. every morning. Set your medication alarm to that time and when it goes off for the first few times, command your dog to get your medication. Thanks to Pavlov's dog, we know that this will trigger a conditioned response (especially with it being at the same time every day because dogs love consistent routine and predictability) and your dog will fetch your medication for you.

- This may take up to a month to be completely consistent so be patient and help your dog when he gets stuck. Every reward for this should be a *large* jackpot, and for a while, it should be the only jackpot of higher value. This means any other jackpot s/he gets should be only more of his regular reward, not a better different food altogether.

Retrieve Items from Store Shelf: If you are wheelchair bound, it may be difficult for you to reach top shelf items at the store and even at home. Luckily, if your service dog is tall enough s/he can do this for you! You'll have to use a shelf at home (I suggest clearing it out first) and add item s/he will be retrieving often.

- Start on a low shelf, about eye-level with your dog. Ask him/her to retrieve it. If s/he has trouble with this, start lower or at a closer distance to you.

- Slowly raise the item higher up on the shelf. Jackpot for being gentle as this will be used at stores.

- Once s/he is proficient with this item at the highest s/he can reach, switch to a different item and repeat the steps.

- Start on the low shelf and slowly move it to the stop. And then switch to another item.

- Any items will do, the more different and random the better. Try a small lightweight book, stand it up, so it is vertical with the bind facing out.

- **Troubleshooting:** If s/he is having trouble gripping the book, let it hang off of the edge a little bit on its side at first. Raise it up the shelf levels and then bring it back down and turn it vertical letting it hang off the edge. All the way up the shelf, and then start over with it vertical pushed back further. Pointing will also be a huge help to your dog as a visual cue when you go to the store to do this.

- Move to a heavier book once s/he is doing well with the lighter book.

- Next, try using items commonly found in the store. Bonus points for items you will find on the top shelf that you regularly buy. The idea is to get them used to what they will be doing in the store as much as possible. Try this in different rooms and at friends' and family's houses first if you can.

- When you feel confident, it's time to go to the store and test it out!

- Be calm and relaxed, if you are not, do not try it that day.

- Bring a few items your dog recognizes from the shelf exercise at home.

- Find a secluded low foot traffic area of the store and place one of the items on a low shelf. Slowly start putting it on higher shelves and in different areas. Jackpot any progress or anything that impresses you.

- Begin asking your dog to retrieve store items on low shelves. Do this for a short while and then leave the store. It is not recommended you do this while you actually need to shop. All of your energy should be going to your dog while he is learning this complicated task.

- The next time you go back start on the low shelf and then ask him/her to get items off a slightly higher shelf and just practice this for this trip. Jackpot at the end.

- Continue this each trip until s/he is getting items off the top shelf! You can give different items names as well, but for the purposes of explaining the action, it was not incorporated. I suggest sticking to one item at a time if you plan on doing this.

Putting store items in the cart: Now that you've gotten your items off of the shelf, it is time to deposit them in the shopping cart. You will find this similar to the laundry basket task with some slight variations.

- First, get the same laundry basket you used before. Give your starting phrase and then put it slightly higher than usual. Perhaps on a stack of books or a low coffee table.

- Use an item that your dog has the most success with when performing the shelf task and set your dog up about a foot from the basket.

- Ask your dog to put the item in the basket. If s/he struggles with this, put the basket on the ground for a few repetitions.

- Try this with a few different items and then begin raising the basket higher.

- Your goal should be to get the basket as high as a shopping cart.

- Next, you will need to find a noticeably different basket. The more variety of baskets or bins you use for this exercise the easier it will be when you do this in public at the store. On that note, you should also practice this in different rooms and even other people's houses if you are able to.

- Once your dog is placing the item in the raised basket, you point to we can move to the next level.

- Place a familiar item on a surface near the lowered basket.

- Ask your dog to bring it to the basket, point to the item you want them to pick up and say "bring" then once they do, point to the basket and say "basket,"

- Try this with a few different items.

- Next, place the item on the shelf you originally used to train the shelf task do the same. The basket should be relatively close to the shelf. Point to the item and say "bring" then, point to the basket and say "basket." Pretty straightforward.

- After completing this to a point of 100% consistent accuracy, you may continue to incrementally add height to the shelf.

- Try moving the basket around so that for each repetition it is in a different spot.

- Then, start adding height to the basket(s).

- Vary the items as well. The more consistently inconsistent you are, the better. As explained earlier, this means the way you teach it should remain the same but certain factors are at random. In this instance, the variables are the height of the basket, the height of the items, and items themselves and the distance between the basket and the shelf.

- Once s/he is retrieving the items off the top shelf and depositing them in the raised basket, you can add distance from the shelf to the basket.

- When you feel confident in your dog's ability to do this task on different shelves with different baskets in different places it is time to go to the store!

- I suggest first using one of those handheld plastic baskets first and choosing items off of the bottom shelf.

- **Troubleshooting:** If s/he is confused, either leave and continue at home or use a familiar item for your dog to take off the shelf. Reward them if they take an item off the shelf but get confused about where to put it and jackpot then for despising of it in the basket.

- **Troubleshooting:** You can also choose to just ask your dog to take an item from you and put it in the basket at the store. This will break it down even further for your dog.

Handing Cash or Credit Cards to the Cashier: Now that all your items have been loaded into the cart, it is time to go check out! However, your wheelchair is restricting your ability to hand the cashier your money, what will you do? Utilize your handy dandy service dog, of course!

- For this lesson you will need an expired credit card, Monopoly or toy money/paper, and a competent helper.

- Begin with your starting phrase.

- Have your helper across from your dog, and you should be in the middle but off to the side.

- For the purposes of explaining, I will be saying credit card as the item you are using. You may use your whole wallet, purse or cash.

- Hand your credit card (use an expired card first so that if it gets damaged during training, it does not matter) to your dog and then have your helper take the card from your dog. *Click* and reward as soon as your helper takes the card.

- Repeat this until you can see your dog catching on to the pattern.

- Next, do the same thing for three repetitions and then for the fourth repetition have your helper wait. It may take a while, but your dog should make a head motion towards the helper. If s/he makes this connection, *click* and jackpot!

- **Troubleshooting:** If it works for your dog, you can have your helper say "bring" in order to bridge the task.

- Once your dog understands the exchange, you and your helper can start to build distance between each other.

- Now you can play pass the card. Have your dog take the card from you, give it to your helper, and then bring it back. Give your dog a reward for bringing it to the helper, jackpot for completing the task by bringing it back to you. But remember, you should be the only one rewarding. Your dog should hand the card to the helper, and then you *click* and your dog should come back to you to receive the reward. Then your helper can entice your dog to come backhand your dog the card and then you can say "bring" and jackpot your dog for returning the card.

- Next, close the distance between you and your helper and put a low table or other surface between you. The dog must reach over the table to give the card.

- Once your dog is proficiently navigating this obstacle, raise the surface. Continue to do this incrementally until the surface is at counter level.

- When you go to the store, inform your cashier that this task is still in the beginning stages. They will be understanding and will help in any way your dog needs.

- To raise your odds of success, don't use the same helper every time. This will prepare your dog for handing objects to strangers.

Finding Your Car: Now you've paid for your groceries and loaded them into your cart. Time to go bring them to the car. But wait! You suffer from memory loss and impaired sight, where is your car? Don't fret, you can train your dog to find your specific car! You will need your touch tape for this!

- Start by your car in your driveway. Announce to your dog your starting phrase.

- Place a piece of tape anywhere on the car that is eye-level to your dog.

- Ask your dog to touch the tape. Continue this until s/he is touching consistently every time. Add the phrase "find the car" now.

- Begin to add distance little by little.

- When your dog is doing this rapidly with speed hook his/her leash to him and let him/her drag it behind them.

- Then, start letting him/her bring you to the car while you hold the leash. You control the speed. This may hinder the dog but keep encouraging then to find the car.

- Once your dog is proficiently guiding you to the visible car, go out of view of the car and ask them to "find the car."

- **Troubleshooting:** If your dog is unsure once out of view of the car, go to where you can see the car but be right by the blind, wall, or tree, etc. And jackpot the success. Then go around the corner out of view and try again.

- When your dog is successfully finding the car out of sight, move the car.

- Practice these steps in a parking lot and move the car around to different spaces. Always make it a fun game for your dog!

Carrying in the Groceries: Finally, you're home and now need to bring in the groceries you and your dog have picked out and bought together! By now, your dog effortlessly carries items to you, but what about carrying them for you. Some people need help carrying grocery bags or perhaps your purse. For this guide, we will be teaching your dog how to carry a reusable grocery bag. If you don't have one, you can purchase one for under a dollar at any grocery store. Not only are they great for the environment, but they are also easier for your dog to hold!

- Have your dog on leash.

- Present to them the empty grocery bag by holding the side of the handle in front of them.

- Ask your dog to "hold" the handle. *Click* and reward.

- Next reward duration. Once you have built duration with the grocery bag, you are ready to put your dog in motion.

- With your dog in front of you take one step back while they are holding the empty bag. Use the leash to guide your dog to walk with you.

- As soon as s/he takes one step say, "Good" and *click* and jackpot the milestone.

- Remember, take hold of the bag before you give your dog the marker.

- Continue this step until you can walk about five steps backward.

- Now it is time to challenge your dog's proprioception. Move to the side of your dog and ask him/her to hold the handle.

- **Troubleshooting:** If s/he tries to swing around to the front of you, try using a wall or some sort of barrier in order to stop this.

- Once s/he is capable of staying on your side and holding the bag for about five seconds, take one step and then *click* and jackpot.

- Build the steps just as you did when s/he was walking in front of you. Remember, if your dog is not in the mood to learn put him/her up in their crate and take them out a few minutes later. Be happy and encouraging for your dog.

Assisting in Transportation: When you go to sleep at night and move from your wheelchair to your bed, you may need help in the transition. Luckily with this in mind during selection, you chose a dog that is suitable for this task in that s/he is sturdy and strong. However, some dogs may not understand your needs, and because of this, they must be trained to accept your weight as you move from point A to point B.

- Begin with your starting phrase.

- Place your hand on your dog's back between his/her shoulder blades.

- *Click* and reward.

- Incrementally increase the amount of pressure you apply and jackpot your dog each time you progress.

- Have your dog on leash and walk with him/her a few steps with your hand lightly on his/her back. Reward small steps and then start rewarding duration and longer distances.

- Gradually add steady pressure and reward him/her for accepting it.

- **Troubleshooting:** If your dog tries to leave your side to alleviate the pressure, go back to the pressure they were comfortable with before. Continue with this pressure until they are comfortable and then add the pressure slower this time.

- Now try it from your chair. Apply slight pressure with your hand on the dog's back. *Click* and reward.

- Continue to add pressure and *click* as soon as you lift yourself up even just a little bit. Jackpot your wonderful dog.

- Do this repetition about five times and then lift yourself up a little more. *Click* and jackpot.

- Steadily increase the pressure as you slowly stand up using your dog as a crutch or cane.

- Combine the two. Get up from your wheelchair and use your dog to walk to your bed. Mission complete! Jackpot your dog!

Moving Paralyzed Limbs in Bed: If your lower extremities are paralyzed, getting into bed and comfortable can be a tedious task. With the help of your service dog, this can go by a little faster and cause you less headache.

- Begin fully in bed without the covers on.

- Have your dog on the side of the bed that you will be getting into every night.

- With a piece of food, lure your dog's nose underneath your leg where s/he should push (often the upper calf).

- Do this by weaving your hand underneath your leg from the inside of your calf to the outside.

- Reward good intentions when your dog touches your leg.

- Continuing to reward this and then withholding the treat a little bit longer will make your dog push harder. This is good.

- Next, begin to lure your dog's nose up once it is under your leg. Jackpot if s/he left your leg even just a little higher.

- Continue this until you can successfully take away the luring. Be patient.

- Once s/he is consistently pushing your leg up with his/her nose without guidance you can drop one leg off the side of the bed and lure your dog's nose under the calf the same way you did before.

- Jackpot your dog for strong pushes.

- Continue this, asking for more every few repetitions by withholding the treat to build frustration which will cause your dog to push harder.

- When s/he can successfully push on leg up, try the second leg.

Wake up Handler: Now you have gone to bed, but unfortunately you suffer from hypersomnia. This means you could sleep well into the day, straight through alarms and miss appointments, medications, or worse – dog training! Fortunately, your service dog can be trained to routinely wake you up. For this, you may get a little messy. You will need peanut butter or honey depending on your preference and possible allergens.

- Begin the session with your starting phrase.

- With your dog next to you take a small fingertip of your chosen yummy treat and smear it on your neck or cheek. Either give your dog a command or choose the alarm sound of your choice. (It should be different than the sound you chose for your medication alarm)

- Do not allow your dog to lick you before the alarm plays.

- Click when the alarm plays, point to the mess and let them self-reward off of your face or neck.

- Do this a few times until your dog understands the order of events.

- Wash your face.

- Play the alarm again and *click*. You can help your dog out by pointing to where you want them to lick. It should be the same place the yummy substance was before.

- Once they are doing this, *click* for the lick (rhymes) and reward from your hand.

- Remove the pointing. If your dog gets confused, practice three repetitions with the pointing guide and do not point for the fourth repetition.

- Create distance between you and the dog.

- Play the alarm, if your dog comes and licks you, jackpot!

- If they are having trouble, stay at that distance but point to your face or neck again.

- Next, lay down in bed and practice your repetitions at a short distance then add a greater distance.

- Once s/he is an expert at this task, start playing the alarm when s/he is sleeping. When s/he wakes up, point to your cheek and jackpot that amazing progress!

- Continue to do this until you feel confident to let the alar him plays routinely in the morning!

Interrupting Self Hitting: Many people who suffer from repetitive behaviors will often times try to control the urges. This can build up and eventually burst into violent acts often on one's self. This outlet can be dangerous and cause injury to the individual. If you suffer from this or something similar, these guided task steps could improve your quality of life tremendously! Remember the game in which you had your dog paw at your hands to reveal the reward? Now it is time to put it to good use!

- Begin with your starting phrase.

- Recap with your dog the same game we learned before.

- Hold one of your hands out with food hidden inside your fist.

- With your other hand hold the clicker.

- The food will always come from the hand they are pawing at, at the beginning. It is okay to switch up hands. In fact, I encourage it.

- Once your dog is proficiently pawing at your hand, withhold the marker. The idea is to get them to continuously paw at your hand until you mark the behavior.

- When you have reached this goal, begin raising your hand towards your face. Do this slowly. Do not jump straight to asking your dog to paw at your hand in a completely new position.

- By moving your hand incrementally, your dog will not notice the difference as much.

- Do not move on to the next increment until your dog is consistently pawing at your hand continuously.

- Once you have gotten your hand all the way to your face, *click* and jackpot your dog's success.

- Continue to reward this for a few lessons.

- When you feel confident, slowly start tapping your face. If your dog sees the same picture every time, it will be easier. With that being said, do three consistently successful repetitions of the previous picture where your hand is only raised and stagnant at your face, then slowly move your hand back and forth in a slow tapping or knocking motion on the fourth repetition.

- Once your dog is doing this with accuracy and not stopping until s/he hears a marker word/sound, speed up the movement. (**Do not** actually touch your face when you start to speed up). Jackpot any progress!

- If your dog is catching on nicely, you can begin giving him/her this picture randomly throughout the day. Make sure you have food on you to reward him/her if s/he does perform the work.

- Many people add licking to this as they feel it adds comfort. You can also apply the deep pressure therapy task to this as well and have your dog lay on your chest and arms. This will provide warmth and security.

- **Troubleshooting:** If your dog does not understand the picture outside of training, keep your lesson shorter and jackpot more frequently.

Conclusion

Congratulations! You have completed the book. You are now in the perfect position to successfully pass the ADI Public Access Test! After this test, you and your dog will be a certified service dog team! I hope you enjoyed your journey with your dog and the memories you have made along the way. No matter what disability you have, the bond that you share with your furry partner shines bright and will provide security and comfortability while promoting independence and strength. You can thank not only your dog but also yourself for the feats you have accomplished. Attribute your new quality of life to the dedicated work you have put into your dog, your new best friend. On the road from here on out, you and your best friend will hit highs and lows. Appreciate the lows at the moment as you look forward to the highs. Just as every moment is a teaching moment for our dogs, it is also a teaching moment for us. As much as you have taught your dog, think back to what s/he has taught you. Patience, understanding, creativity, connection, and above all else your dog has and will continue to teach you about yourself. As a professional dog trainer, the best life lessons I have learned are from the dogs I have trained. They will reveal your flaws and reflect them back towards you forcing you to confront them. Once you do, you will see a spike in your communication and bond between you and your dog. The more aware you are of these inevitable speed bumps during your continuous training, the better you will understand how to simplify and solve issues when they arise. Have a wonderful and fulfilling journey and do not hesitate to reread any section of the book over again for maintenance. Remember, the training never ends.

Finally, if you found this book useful in any way, a review on Amazon is always appreciated!

Often times, the people that need help the most are unable afford the training needed to go into a service dog. Sa there are many factors that a lot of people may be unaw of when attempting to train their own. This book is here to guide y down this journey. The benefits of training your own dog are pricel if you sufficiently follow the rules and steps outlined in this book. following the guidance in this book, you are accepting an unbreaka bond you will create between you and your service dog – a bond t will mitigate your disability and award you with daily independence.

Inside the book, you will learn everything you need to know about t laws that allow you to own and utilize your service dog. You will well versed in how to properly assess and select a service dog, wl type of service dog is best for you, and the ins and outs of why t selection process is so strict. You will also learn how to capture a keep your dog's attention even under high distraction and build t unbreakable bond. And most importantly, this book will help y build your dog's obedience – the very foundation that will make yc dog the best service dog ever.

This book will not leave you hanging when it is time to bring your w mannered companion out to the town to apply everything you learned and prepared for the access test. Finally, and arguably t most exciting part, teaching your dog the tasks that will gain you tl independence! No matter your disability there is something everyone in here. Read this book thoroughly, follow the step-by-st guides, and apply the lessons properly, then you and your dog v excel together!

Training Your Psychiatric Service Dog:

Step-By-Step Guide to an Obedient Psychiatric Service Dog

Table of Contents

Introduction

Congratulations on downloading *Training Your Psychiatric Service Dog*. You are taking that first step to live a life with more freedom and mobility. A Psychiatric Service Dog allows you the ability to be more interactive within the world. It gives you the freedom to move about with the assistance that you need to have a fulfilling life.

They say that a dog is man's best friend, and I honestly believe that with the proper training, a dog can save a person's life. The dogs that are used as Psychiatric Service dogs are trained to be your best friend and your medical medium. They are trained to know what is going on in your life before you ever know what is going on. They are trained to be highly skilled at maintaining your health.

This book is designed to give you the tools that are needed for you to train your dog to be as skilled as any other Psychiatric Service dog. Even though I broke each training session into a specific diagnoses-based need, they can all be used to provide you with freedoms that you never thought were possible. Do not let your diagnosis get in the way of starting a new chapter in your life. Disability does not have to be the end of your life. It can be the beginning of a beautiful friendship between you and your Psychiatric Service animal.

The following chapters will discuss all the necessary steps that must be taken in training your own Psychiatric Service Dog. There are many skills and techniques in training a dog and each one of these can provide you with more freedom and flexibility in your life. Psychiatric Service Dogs provide you the comfort of knowing that you can experience life and all its adventures without concerning yourself with those annoying disabilities that have been limiting you. Many people have found that with a Psychiatric Service Dog, they are able to spend more time out in the world enjoying concerts, restaurants, driving, and many other activities.

This is the book that will give you that freedom and peace of mind. Start training your Psychiatric Service Dog and begin enjoying life again in as little as 6 weeks.

There are plenty of books on this subject on the market, so thanks again for choosing this one! Every effort was made to ensure it is full of as much useful information as possible. Please enjoy!

Chapter 1: What is a Psychiatric Service Dog?

Psychiatric Service Dogs are not a pet, but a medical necessity for those who are suffering from severe Psychiatric Disorders. A Psychiatric Service Dog is a dog that is specially trained to provide a service for someone who suffers from a Psychiatric Disorder.

*No copyright infringement intended

If you have a Psychiatric disorder, then you are well aware of what one is. If you do not have a Psychiatric disorder, then a little bit of information should help you understand if you have one. A psychiatric disorder is a disorder that is related to mental health. This can include anything from Anxiety, PTSD, Autism, Depression, Schizophrenia, and much more. If you have a disorder that limits your ability to live a fulfilling life, then you may need a Psychiatric Service Dog.

A Psychiatric Service Dog helps those with disabilities survive in a world that is unfriendly to them. It provides them with the ability to have life experiences that they would otherwise not have been able to due to their disabilities. They are able to have adventures and live a life without concern for whether or not they are going to have an episode.

Psychiatric Service Dogs are trained for many different services to assist the disabled in their daily activities as well as handling their episodes from their disabilities. These can be anything from alerting the owner to medication times, finding a lost item, checking the environment for triggers, recognizing an anxiety attack coming on, blocking the owner from being approached by others, calming them when in an episode, and many more services.

In this book, I will talk about what tasks are available for you to train your Psychiatric Service Dog to do, which types of dogs are best to train, the best age to start training a dog, different equipment that will help you with your Psychiatric Service Dog, the government rules and regulations for Psychiatric Service Dogs, what your Psychiatric Service Dog needs to know to qualify as a Psychiatric service dog, and a step-by-step guide on how to train for specific conditions.

*No copyright infringement intended

What are the Roles that Psychiatric Service Dogs play in the Lives of a Disabled Person?

A disabled person that has a psychiatric disability which limits their access to living a fulfilled life can be better served by having a Psychiatric Service Dog as a companion. This can open up doors for them that they never imagined and allow them to experience life without limitations. Psychiatric Service Dogs are specifically trained to perform tasks that allow this to happen.

As a Psychiatric Service Dog, the training can be intense and specific to their handler's needs. They must adhere to a higher standard of training and be able to handle many more things with diplomacy. For instance, a Psychiatric Service Dog needs to be able to enter a crowded area without being bothered by other animals or people. This is something that they must be trained to do. Most dogs will not handle other animals in their space easily. However, as a Psychiatric Service Dog, they need to act as if that other animal is not even there. Psychiatric Service Dogs provide such services listed below:

• Answering the door for their handler if they are unable to do that. They do this by pulling a lever or, if the house is fitted specifically for this service, by applying pressure a part of the door where it can be opened.

• Picking things up and bringing them to the handler such as medication, something they dropped or the mail.

• Alerts others to the handler in times of extra assistance from a caretaker. This is a way of alerting the nurse or caretaker that the disabled person needs their services.

• Provides mobility support as well as the ability to climb stairs, get up off of furniture, and navigate tight areas or areas with limited visibility. This is done by leading the handler with a strong lead or leash. This can help them when out in public or at home.

• Providing stability and support for those that have imbalance issues is another way that a Psychiatric Service Dog can help their handler. Many dogs provide this service for those that are arthritic, have equilibrium issues or even stroke victims.

• Provides a saddle bag for the handler and carries medicine, diabetic supplies, anxiety supplies, and such. This allows the handler to have access to leaving their home without having to worry about carrying their medical needs with them.

Psychiatric Service Dogs can also provide services for their handlers in times of emergency such as:

•   Retrieves the phone for the handler when they need to contact 911 or a family member for help, as well as pushing an alert button when the handler needs service.

•   Barks into the speakerphone for emergency services to know that the handler is either in danger or needs emergency services. This is a way for the emergency services to know that the person in need is not only disabled but also in need of assistance.

•   Responds to the handler in appropriate ways to interrupt or alert them to a psychiatric episode or occurrence. This helps the handler know that an episode is coming or helps pull them out of an episode that could potentially cause them more pain or struggle.

•   Provides an alarm for the handler when they are having an episode or in distress so that other people will be aware of the episode. This allows them to get help for their handler and provide the necessary medical treatment that their handler needs.

•   When experiencing a seizure or anxiety episode, they will alert others to you and bring them over, so they can assist you in your needs. This works great for when you are down on the floor with an episode, seizure or suicide attempt. This is especially helpful for those that suffer from severe depression, mood disorders, anxiety, and seizures.

•   Uses a system to alert the handler and the fire department or neighbors to a fire, burglary or other issues that would require the handler to evacuate the home or call the police.

*No copyright infringement intended

These are all the services that allow the handler or disabled person the ability to live their lives without fear of what would happen during these situations. These are just a few of the services that can be provided by a Psychiatric Service Dog. There are so many ways that a Psychiatric Service Dog can modify or help a disabled person's life. With a Psychiatric Service Dog, the disabled person is able to feel more confident in themselves and their abilities to live alone or explore their towns or take a vacation without needing a constant caretaker or nurse on call.

•   As a Psychiatric Service Dog, their role is to provide the disabled handler with the freedoms and luxuries that others get to enjoy.

•   They help to aid them with episodes of disassociation with the surrounding area. They also provide the handler with the ability to have stability when they are disoriented due to medications.

- They can provide the handler with an alert that will inform them that it is time to take medication.

- Often times, when people are having anxiety, panic attacks or episodes, they need a tactile stimulation that will bring them out of those episodes or help them be aware of when the episode is coming on. The Psychiatric Service Dog is trained to provide these services.

- They are also trained to recognize when someone is hallucinating and how to handle them when they come.

- For those handlers that are experiencing PTSD from being attacked or being at war, they can benefit from having a Psychiatric Service Dog. This dog can provide them with someone that checks every room before they enter, and alert them if everything is okay or not in the room.

- If someone has the potential to self-harm or has self-harmed in the past, then a Psychiatric Service Dog will provide them with interruption to these behaviors. This will help those that are OCD about these behaviors.

With all these services that a Psychiatric Service Dog can provide, you can see the benefits that they could give to the lives of disabled people. Many U. S. Veterans are looking for assistance in medical stabilization after returning from war and a Psychiatric Service Dog can be the key to providing them the stability in their medical treatment that they need outside of medication and counseling.

*No copyright infringement intended

By caring for a Psychiatric Service Dog, it provides them the necessary reasons to take care of themselves and another living with them. This, oftentimes, can provide them with a purpose and a means for leaving their house. This allows the opportunity to go outside and have interactions with others, as well as provide them with a reason for leaving their comfort zone and experiencing more things in life.

When people with depression think of leaving their homes, they are not too thrilled about the idea. Having a Psychiatric Service Dog will provide them with a reason to get out of bed and get fresh air. Fresh air and sunlight provide Vitamin D which is a vital nutrient that is needed for us to be happy and can increase our moods. Fresh air has been known to reverse the effects of depression as well as the symptoms that depressed people experience. This is also something that can be provided to a handler through an Emotional Support Animal. Through scientific and clinical studies, people with disabilities have expressed a greater rate of self-esteem, independence as well as happiness when living with a service animal or emotional support animal.

One dog is capable of helping over 60 people. Through programs that allow Veterans to train a Psychiatric Service Dog, they not only train the dog how to serve but heal themselves by giving them a purpose. This helps them cope with PTSD and other issues. They help reduce the anxiety of the handler so that they can sleep better which in turn helps them improve their health. By training the dog to experience new environments, the handler is, in turn, bringing themselves out of the isolation that many people who suffer PTSD or depressed will place themselves in. When the veterans train the dog that they can trust the world and that it is a safe spot to be in, they are also learning this lesson themselves.

Psychiatric Service Dogs provide a boost of confidence for children as well as adults that suffer from Psychiatric disorders. There have been several research studies that have proven that a Psychiatric Service Dog helps release the dopamine levels or oxytocin levels within the handler. These two levels are related to stabilizing the moods and helping the wellbeing of the handler. Children who have confidence issues or autism can use a Psychiatric Service Dog to feel more confident when having to engage with other people. It teaches them to interact with the dog which helps them to learn how to interact with other people.

Although the training for a Psychiatric Service Dog can be super specific and intense, the benefit far outweighs the expense of time or money that is put into it. It can take weeks to months to train a Psychiatric Service Dog depending on the training that is needed and the dog's ability to adapt to the tasks that are being asked of them—but do not fear. This is something you can do yourself, by applying the techniques in this book.

*No copyright infringement intended

In the next chapter, I will discuss the necessary skills that are needed to become a Psychiatric Service Dog, and how to ensure that your dog will have these skills. The rest of this book will focus on choosing the right dog for the task as well as the choice of equipment for your dog to adapt to your needs. I will also discuss the laws that regulate what you can and cannot do with your Psychiatric Service Dog, and the necessary role your dog must play when out in public. The last part of this book will focus on training techniques for specific services that your Psychiatric Service Dog will need to be able to perform for your needs.

Chapter 2: What Are the Necessary Skills Needed To Be a Psychiatric Service Dog?

There are a few necessary skills that your dog must have to be a Psychiatric Service Dog. Each one of these skills is to ensure that your dog is being of service to you in the best feasible way. Each skill set is used to determine if this is the right dog for your needs and if they are able to acquire the training that is necessary for you.

In order for a dog to be a viable choice for a Psychiatric Service Dog, they must exhibit what some people call the Good Companion Training. With Good Companion Training, your dog will learn how to be obedient to you. Since every dog is different, this can mean different things for each dog. A dog with this training will not jump on others, bark or growl when not appropriate, not dig in the yard, or climb on the furniture if you do not want them to. They will not chew on something they are not supposed to or bite others. They will not eat off others plates or snatch things out of babies' hands. These are considered basic obedience training steps. A few of the things that are involved with basic obedience are listed below.

- Being able to heel or slow their pace when the handler has slowed, stopped, or made a certain sound or movement, as well as they heel when released off the leash when given a specific command and not resume walking until told to.

- Another skill is being able to stand perfectly still while the vet or handler examines the dog for a check-up. Sometimes, we need to examine our pets to see if something is bothering them, or the vet needs them to be still for exams. This is a necessary skill to have.

- When the handler has released the Psychiatric Service Dog from the leash, the dog needs to be able to stay close to the handler and return to the handler with a simple command if sent to retrieve something.

•   Another obedience skill that the dog needs to have is to be able to sit for over 1 minute without moving from the spot. This is to ensure that the dog can follow the command of sit and stay.

•   *No copyright infringement intended

•   Along the same lines of sit and stay is the down and stay skill that is also necessary for a Psychiatric Service Dog. When out in public, your Psychiatric Service Dog needs to be able to sit for over 3 minutes while you eat, change clothes, check out at the register, use the restroom, and much more. They must be able to stay without getting up or losing focus.

•   Dropping something or giving something to you on command is an important part of obedience skills. Being able to command your dog to drop it or give it to you can mean the difference between a Psychiatric Service Dog that collects things and brings them to you and one that does not.

•   Another obedience skill that is useful to have is to be able to follow hand signals without voice commands. Some disabled people cannot speak, and this can be confusing for a dog that has learned with auditory commands. In this instance, the Psychiatric Service dog would need to be able to respond to hand signals instead of auditory signals.

•   Another thing that a dog should learn is to retrieve and return. This means that the dog should be able to leave the handler, retrieve something that was dropped or needed from a distance and return the item to the handler.

•   The dog should also be able to ignore sudden loud or strange noises that can arise. When a dog startles easily with noise or strange sounds this can be a problem. The Psychiatric Service Dog should not alert or respond to anything that the handler has not said or done.

• Another thing that goes along with this is that they should be able to walk on unfamiliar surfaces without being uncomfortable. Often times, a new surface will startle a dog or create an anxiety about being on it. The Psychiatric Service Dog should be comfortable approaching or walking on any surface it comes in contact with.

*No copyright infringement intended

• Psychiatric Service Dogs should be comfortable around people who have canes, wheelchairs, children, strangers, and also those that create loud noises like the mentally-challenged individuals. They should not respond to other people, but instead, act as if they are not there unless told by the owner that it is ok.

• Another part of this would be not alerting to other animals. Since dogs tend to chase cats and small prey or respond to other dogs with interest or disgust, a Psychiatric Service Dog should respond as if the other animals are not there. This ensures that they are focused on their handlers needs instead of losing focus and being distracted.

A great starting point for a dog that is intended to be a Psychiatric Service Dog is to enroll them in the Canine Good Citizen training course. This course is taught to ensure that the dog is a good citizen and it is also a jumping off point to ensure that your choice of Psychiatric Service dog was best suited to you. It trains the dog how to be well-mannered with the other animals, people, and specific situations. Since this is a training course that provides a certification through the American Kennel Club and its approved trainers, this is something that will need to be done by someone certified to teach the course. However, if you adopt a dog from the shelter, often times they will be provided with this training, and it will be included in their bio and their adoption fee.

Some of the training that is provided in this course can include:

*No copyright infringement intended

- Allowing a friendly stranger to approach them and communicate with them.

- Sitting in a polite manner while someone pets them.

- Allowing someone to groom them without aggravation, and also check on their extremities.

- Walking beside their owners with a loose leash without pulling or bolting.

- Passing through a crowd without being bothered by other people or animals.

- Sitting and laying on command and staying for a length of time that the handler decides.

- Coming to the handler when they are called from a distance of 10 feet.

- Showing no reaction or only positive reactions to another dog.

- Responding appropriately to a distraction that is provided by the trainer.

- Staying for extended periods of time without the handler in a supervised separation. This ensures that the dog will not have separation anxiety.

Another crucial factor is that they should have skills that fit within your choice of lifestyle. Often times, a depressed person will spend hours in bed, sometimes even days. The Psychiatric Service Dog that you choose should be able to not potty in the house for the long hours that the handler is in bed, as well as motivate the handler to exit their bed and take them outside for potty times.

Chapter 3: How to Pick the Right Psychiatric Service Dog

By starting off with knowing exactly what you are expecting from your Psychiatric Service Dog, you can begin to find the right dog that is suited for your needs. In order to know exactly what you will need you, should simply ask yourself a few questions.

*No copyright infringement intended

These questions can help you determine your needs and the appropriate dog that will fit these needs. You should also determine what your limitations will be in caring for your chosen Psychiatric Service Dog.

You will need to start with making a list of your Psychiatric Service Dog needs. Ask yourself these questions:

- *What will your Psychiatric Service dog do for you?*

- *How will you train your Psychiatric Service dog to do the tasks that you need?*

Next, list the disabilities that you will need assistance from the Psychiatric Service dog for.

- *Do they need to react to what you react to?*

- *Do they need to be non-reactive?*

- *Do they need to assist you in not engaging in a destructive behavior?*

- *Do you want a redirect or a complete stop of the behavior?*

- *Is there a physical manifestation that will help your dog recognize the issue?*

- *Is the interaction with the dog needed to change your physiology?*

- *Is there another way that the Psychiatric Service Dog can assist you with these issues?*

Next, you will need to discuss with your doctor, or those that are closest to you to determine if they have any ideas or actions that need to be curtailed or stopped. Discuss how your disability has interfered with or impacted your life and if there is something that would be beneficial to what your Psychiatric Service Dog could help with. Discuss with others that own a Psychiatric Service Dog and find out how theirs is helping them in their life or making their life more manageable. Ask if there is something specific that they trained their Psychiatric Service Dog to do that would also benefit you. Then create a list of the things that you will need your Psychiatric Service Dog to do for you to assist you to live a more comfortable life.

Once you get to this point, you will need to specify the size of the breed of dog that you will use. For instance, a dog for balance will need to be large. An average-sized person needs a dog weighing at least 50 pounds for him to be stable. For a larger size person, you may need a bigger dog for stability. If the need is not associated with stability, then a smaller breed dog will be a good option. They need less space in your home, their food intake is minimal, and since they live longer life spans, they will provide you with a longer Psychiatric Service Dog time period. They are a great asset for tactile stimulation and also alerting for behavior modification or episodes.

The next thing that you will need to think of is the personality that you have and the dog's personality. Will you mesh well with specific breeds more than others? If you are thinking of a dog that is naturally inclined to chase down vermin, then they will be more independent than those that are used for retrieving the game that is shot down. A dog breed that is assigned to be guard dogs will need to be handled by someone that is confident with their handling abilities, which means that they would not be an excellent choice for a Psychiatric Service Dog. A toy breed dog is an excellent dog for companionships and Psychiatric Service dogs.

*No copyright infringement intended

Talk to a professional trainer that is specialized in choosing the appropriate dog for a Psychiatric Service Dog based on the needs of the handler and see what they suggest for your needs. The trainer does not have to be a trainer for a Psychiatric Service Dog, any trainer that works with dogs that are trained for agility, competition trainers, sports trainers, as well as search and rescue trainers can be a valuable resource to finding out information on specific breeds that will help you.

Another source of identifying the right breed for your needs is to contact other people who have trained their own Psychiatric service dogs. Get insight on how they chose their dog breed and the methods they used to identify the appropriate breed for their needs.

Now, you should consider your activities every day. Are you active or inactive? A dog will need to have at least one walk a day to explore the world, sniff out the other dogs in the area, and enjoy nature. A Psychiatric Service Dog has needs that are not easily ignored. They will need to potty and have exercise. A family member is an excellent source of getting help with your Psychiatric Service Dog. However, the goal should be for you to get outside and experience the world. There are also several services that will come to your home and walk your dog for you for a fee.

If you do not like lots of activity, then you need to choose a dog that has low-energy levels such as a Shih Tzus or another small dog. A medium energy style dog will need at least one hour or more of continuous exercise each day. This can be a Labrador Retriever or something similar. If you find that a higher energy breed dog is a good option for you, then choose something like a Border Collie or even a Boxer. These types of dogs will need to run for a length of time for at least 1 to 2 hours per day. They thrive within dog sports type of activities and need constant activity to keep busy.

*No copyright infringement intended

If you do not have a lot of active days, then do not try to overestimate the activity within your life. This can only mean disaster or destructive behaviors that can come from boredom. A dog with minimal energy can be over-exercised. However, a dog with extra energy with minimal exercise is going to be disastrous in the long run.

If you enjoyed an active lifestyle prior to your disability such as agility, flyball, dancing, or any other physical stimulation, then choosing a dog that is active in moderation can be a great option as your Psychiatric Service Dog. This will also help you to get outside and be active, giving you back your previous lifestyle prior to the disability.

Second to the last, you will need to consider the grooming required for the dog. Although grooming can be a very therapeutic activity, it is also something that people with arthritis will have struggles with. It does provide a repetitive behavior for someone who finds that they are OCD about actions to have an alternative to replace those behaviors with.

However, there are certain conditions that can be affected severely by the presence of hair or the need to groom a dog. Someone who is in a depressive state may find themselves lethargic and unable to care for the dog's grooming. This can present a problem for the dog's hair and health. On the same note, someone who is OCD about germs and cleanliness may find that a dog's hair or grooming a dog to be overwhelming and disgusting. This can actually create more anxiety in the situation.

*No copyright infringement intended

By deciding what will bother you and what will not bother you with regards to your dog's grooming, you can be better prepared for the necessary upkeep and maintenance. Although every person with the same diagnosis is different, the grooming of a dog is specific to each breed. A long-haired dog will need the same grooming procedures as another long-hair dog will need. So, determine what it is that you are willing to do on a daily basis for your Psychiatric Service Dog before picking the breed that you will use.

A Greyhound or a Pit Bull has a short coat that is smooth and sheds minimally. They do not require copious amounts of grooming. Dogs such as Golden Retrievers, German Shepherds, as well as a Labrador Retriever can have a coat that is either short or medium in length. They tend to shed often and need to be copiously brushed 3 times per week.

A long-coated dog such as a Lhasa Apso as well as a Blue Heeler will need to be brushed often. This will need to be done every day. They will also need a regular grooming appointment at the dog salon to get a haircut. If you have allergies, then the Poodle, Schnauzer, and Bichon Frise will need to be your optimal choice. They do not shed and are hypoallergenic. They will need regular grooming with brushes or combs. They should be groomed every 2 days and have a regular haircut. A mixed breed dog can be quite different and difficult to gauge when it comes to shedding and grooming needs. They will have needs based on the mixture that is in them.

*No copyright infringement intended

Finally, consider your work or home life schedule and as well as the tasks that you are already responsible for. Think about the other people in your life. Think about your home life. Think about your work environment or doctors' offices that you visit. Ask yourself these questions:

- *Are they allergic to dogs?*
- *Do you live in a colder climate or a hotter climate?*
- *Do you visit places that require a quiet environment?*
- *Will it be troublesome to carry a cloth to always wipe up slobber?*
- *Do you live in a small apartment in a big city?*
- *Are you traveling on planes or trains often?*

Now, add up all the answers you received from the questions and find the right dog for you.

Do some research on the dog breeds that meet your needs and begin compiling the pros and cons on which breed is the best one for you. Once you have narrowed it down, go to some breeders and shelters and get a feel for the dog, its mentality, and connection with its handler.

Which dog is best for you and your needs?

Some dogs are specifically bred for their mentality. These dogs would make great Psychiatric Service Dogs.

*No copyright infringement intended

If the person that is handling the dog does not have the ability to brush their own hair, then they should not have a dog that will require copious amounts of grooming. Dogs that require copious amounts of care should only be considered for those handlers that need the motivation to be active in life. For those that need a reassuring and gentle breed, then choosing a dog that is bred for those qualities should be the most important first step.

There are several breeds of dog in the world that would qualify for a Psychiatric Service Dog. These can be anything from a Chihuahua to a Pitbull. Any dog is an acceptable option. However, some dogs that have a specific need would require more time and energy to maintain than others. Knowing what you are needing and looking for is going to be the determining factor in picking the perfect dog.

Below, I will give specific natural qualities to several of the dog breeds that people have been using for Psychiatric Service dogs in the past 10 years. This will give you a base to rate your perfect dog by.

*No copyright infringement intended

Some of the most people-pleasing dog breeds are:

- Beagles
- Cavalier King Charles Spaniel
- Flat-coated Retriever
- Collie
- Pug
- Irish Setter
- French Bulldog
- Bichon Frise
- Bulldog
- Maltese

Dogs that are great for a small to medium-sized house:

- Toy Poodle
- Cavalier King Charles Spaniel
- Pug
- Bichon Frise
- Yorkshire Terrier
- Corgi
- Dachshund

- French Bulldog
- Beagle
- Chihuahua

Dogs that fall under the general area of acceptable Psychiatric Service Dogs:

- Labrador Retriever
- Beagle
- Rottweiler
- Saint Bernard
- Pomeranian
- Standard Poodle
- French Bulldog
- Pug
- Greyhound
- German Shepherd
- Golden Retriever

With all the different breeds that we have listed here, I want to give you some insight into how several of these dogs will provide adequate, if not excellent, help as a Psychiatric Service Dog. To start off, I will discuss the Standard Poodle.

The Standard Poodle

These dogs are very bright and are easily trainable. They have an exceptional ability to pick up quickly on training commands and are especially eager to please the handler. Poodles are widely liked due to their brilliant minds. Because of their original breeding training of retrieval, they have the tenacity for following cues that are given by their handlers for helping those that need someone to pick up and retrieve items for them.

Another positive for poodles as Psychiatric Service Dog is that they have a low shed ratio compared to other dog breeds. This makes for a minimal maintenance Psychiatric Service Dog. The low shedding also means that they have a hypoallergenic coat making them an excellent choice for those with allergies to pets and pet dander.

The Poodle is an affectionate dog that is good-natured, especially with children and disabled individuals. They have been known to excel in obedience training courses and are loyal to their handlers. They are great for those that suffer from depression, anxiety, as well as panic attacks. Since Poodles notice the moods of their handlers, they can know indirectly that their handler is unhappy. This is something that does not have to be taught to them, they are naturally sensitive. After the proper training techniques are taught, they can become attuned deeply to the handler's moods and have a connection to their handler that can help them identify and divert the handler from self-destructive behaviors.

The Havanese

Although the Havanese is a small pooch, they have a highly intelligent characteristic. This allows them to be trainable, making them a suitable selection for Psychiatric Service Dog. They have a friendly personality that helps them be a great family pet choice as well as a great option for children with disabilities. The Havanese is an excellent choice for those that are suffering from depression due to their friendly personalities. They are also outgoing, showering their handler with love and cuddles, which can improve the person's disposition. They thrive on love and enjoy snuggles with their handler. This means that they will be a great companion for someone that suffers from mood disorders.

Because of their sensitivity, they are able to attune themselves to their handler's emotional energy. This allows them to know when their handler is having an emotional episode and they need support or comfort. This also makes them loyal and a great dog for your lap when you need comfort.

They know tricks such as retrieving medications for their owners as well as interrupting the behaviors that can be harmful or repetitive and can be self-destructive. By providing a focal point, a child with Autism is able to bring both the autistic world together with the real world.

*No copyright infringement intended

The Cavalier King Charles Spaniel

They have an enormous personality that makes them very friendly and lovable. They enjoy snuggling and showing affection to their handlers as well as others. They bond strongly with their handler as well as the children within their household. This is where they get the name "Velcro pooch". Because of this, they are an amazing Psychiatric Service Dog for those that suffer from PTSD and depression.

While petting a King Charles Spaniel, the repetition will help create tranquility and calm within their mind. This helps tremendously with those that need a calming activity to help them deal with their disabilities. Cavaliers are not at all aggressive towards people and children. This means that they are a great option for those that need a Psychiatric Service Dog who can be in public without being aggressive to other people and animals. They do need lots of training prior to being used when in public, though. However, this dog's intelligence makes it super easy for them to learn their necessary training commands.

The Cavalier is a very gentle, quiet breed which makes them an excellent breed for PTSD handlers as well as those that suffer from anxiety. They are intuitively linked to their handlers, making it easier for them to identify with the handler and connect with all of their emotional episodes.

*No copyright infringement intended

The Labrador Retriever

The Labrador Retriever has a superior intelligence to other dogs. This makes them an excellent choice for not only Psychiatric Service Dogs but also as great companion animals. They also tend to be very gentle towards their handlers and children.

Since the retriever was originally bred for retrieving, this means they make an excellent Psychiatric Service Dog for those that need help retrieving their mail, as well as picking things up that they have dropped. This shows how their intelligence, eagerness to please, and obedience provide them the capabilities of being a Psychiatric Service dog.

They maintain a stable and balanced personality which helps tremendously with ADHD and ADD children and adults. This also provides them with the necessary temperament for Autistic children and adults. They help the Autistic handler to be calmer and more settled during moments of outbursts. Individuals that are suffering from schizophrenia will also feel safer and secure due to the ability to focus on the care of their dog and the calmness that these dogs provide to the environment.

*No copyright infringement intended

The Miniature Schnauzer

Yet another small breed dog that makes an excellent choice for a Psychiatric Service Dog. This miniature dog is a spirited dog with lots of spunk. They love to romp and play. But they also love to lay and be cuddled. They make a great sidekick for those that need to be more active in life or those that love to be active but need to have the Psychiatric support that the Psychiatric Service Dog will provide.

They have a high intelligence level and learn how to be obedient and a people pleaser fairly easy. They pick-up on social and emotional cues which makes them a great companion for those with emotional instability.

The German Shepherd

Although most people think these dogs make superb police dogs, they do not realize that they can make excellent Psychiatric Support or Psychiatric Service Dogs as well. The German Shepherd is a very tenacious and smart dog breed with the discipline to learn all they are taught. They are eager to please their handlers and love to show affection. They perform remarkably when asked to and this is no different when the disabled person needs help from them. This can make them a great asset for handlers that have mental health issues.

Because of all the natural character traits of the German Shepherd, they make an excellent choice for those suffering from OCD symptoms as well as anxiety issues. If trained properly, they will be able to detect when their handler is having a panic attack or onset of a panic attack, and then prevent the panic attack from coming on. They can be trained to interrupt the behaviors with a pawing technique that will redirect the handler to a new behavior or action.

*No copyright infringement intended

The gentleness of the breed and the loyalty they exhibit towards their handlers makes them a great dog for PTSD sufferers. They are an excellent choice for searching homes for any signs of unsafe people or activities. They are easy to train due to their ability to process knowledge quickly and have a similar intelligence level to humans. They provide a calming environment and can be depended on for moral support as well as provide safety.

The Lhasa Apso

The Lhasa Apso is a breed that has natural instincts that alert people of intruders. This means they make great Psychiatric Service Dogs for those that need an alert dog for specific triggers or behaviors. They will make great companions as well as Psychiatric Service Dogs for those dealing with PTSD, as well as bipolar disorder and depression.

They have a cheerful disposition and will put a smile on anyone's face. This makes them a great option for calming and cheering up those that are depressed. They also have an uncanny knack for helping identify the different moods that their handler will display during a bipolar episode, and through training, they can learn how to react in an appropriate manner such as nudging the handler to alert them of the change in moods. This will place the handler back on course for the right mood.

*No copyright infringement intended

They tend to be comical and entertaining, which helps them uplift the moral of those that are depressed or bipolar. This makes them an excellent source of companionship with those that deal with mood disabilities.

Now that I have given you a few insights into how to pick a good Psychiatric Service Dog, the rest of this chapter will assist you in whether you should get a shelter dog or a pure breed dog, and if you should start with a puppy or an adult dog.

Shelter dog vs. pure breed dog

Shelter dogs come in all shapes and sizes. Some of the dogs that you can find within the shelter are, believe it or not, actually pure-bred dogs that have been left by their owners due to housing or financial circumstances. So, what you might find out about shelter dogs is that they can actually be pure-bred dogs, as well as mutts.

*No copyright infringement intended

Breeders are able to provide you with a medical history and family bloodline for the dog that you are considering using as a Psychiatric Service Dog. This information can be useful for not only the genetic history of the dog but also for the personal information so that you will know if the temperament is ideal for your needs. When you examine the bloodline of the dog that you are choosing, you will be aware of any genetic medical issues that can affect your dog. This helps you know if the dog breed that you are choosing will have continuous issues with their hips or other genetic issues. Within dogs, personalities are inherited and passed down. This can be troublesome when picking out a shelter dog since you do not have any genetic background or know the parents of the dog that you are picking out.

If the background of the dog's family tree is riddled with Psychiatric Service dogs, genetically, the dog will be an excellent choice for a Psychiatric Service dog as well. If need a dog that provides stability, then you will need to ensure that your Psychiatric Service Dog does not have a predisposition for hip dysplasia or joint pains. Running a genetic test will help you to know these details about the dogs that you are choosing between.

*No copyright infringement intended

A breeder will charge more for a dog that is a purebred with a great genetic background. Although this can be expensive from the beginning, it can end up costing you much less in the long run. Especially if you have obtained a shelter dog that needs 2 hip replacements.

Although a rescue or shelter dog may seem like a great idea in the beginning, they can cost more money in the long run if they have health conditions that need to be maintained. They can also become bonded too intensely to their new owners and this can create a separation anxiety which can be exceedingly difficult to deal with. Rescue centers and shelters offer a very inexpensive way to obtain a dog that can be trained for Psychiatric Service Dogs. Most the dogs that come from a shelter or rescue have already been fixed, they have had all their basic veterinarian needs to be met and have often times been tested for temperament as well as good citizenship. They are a much bigger risk in the genetic history and medical background since they are shelter or rescue pups.

A breakdown of how much a rescue or shelter dog and a pure-bred dog, can cost you is listed below for you to understand the difference in cost.

Rescued Adult already altered dog:

Adoption fee: $120

Veterinarian bills for genetic issues or health: $2000

Training cost of hiring out a trainer: $2000

Service Dog Gear: $100

Food and accessories: $1000

Grand Total: $5220

*No copyright infringement intended

Dog Purchased from a Service Dog Breeder:
Purchase price: $2500

Veterinarian Bills: $750

Expenses for Training with a Trainer: $1100

Service Dog Gear: $100

Food and accessories: $1000

End Total: $5450

Even though the purchase price of a rescue or shelter dog is slightly less, the continued cost in the long run for medical expenses will drastically change this. The training cost will also be very different since, in the end, you will have to continuously train the shelter dog when new behaviors arise or to modify a negative behavior that will hinder your ability to train them at first. So, starting with a purebred dog from the beginning could only cost you the initial fees that are needed, instead of a continuous vet bill and retraining bill.

Remember that the dog you chose should be right for you and your needs. It should be as healthy as possible and have a lifespan that will give you the most benefit for the cost that you have put into it. You also need to remember that dogs that have unknown genetic backgrounds or are shelter dogs above the age of 3, can potentially have a reduced lifespan based on the genetic makeup as well as the amount of life left in them.

*No copyright infringement intended

Puppy vs. Adult dog

Now that I have explained the differences between using a shelter dog versus a purebred dog, you will be wondering if you need a pup or an adult. As with shelter or pure-bred dogs, you will need to decide based on your needs and what you want. A pup can be a wonderful experience if you are emotionally and physically ready to take care of a pup. However, if you are not, then you will need to get an adult dog. With a pup, you are able to watch as it grows and learns, seeing every milestone as they come around. With an adult, this has already taken place and you may miss some of the fun and cute puppy stages. A puppy will also need to be trained in how to potty outside. This means lots of time spent crate training the new pup. Socialization is also necessary for a new pup as well. They will need to be introduced to other pups, so they know how to play and not be aggressive toward other animals or people. Puppies tend to chew on everything and training them not to chew can cost you time, money, and aggravation. Consider these when you are deciding on picking a pup or an adult dog.

Often times, you will find an adult dog is more stable in their personalities and they are not in the chewing stages anymore. They tend to be well potty trained and know basic obedience. This gives them an advantage above a puppy, especially since puppies need all the extra work before they can start to be trained for Psychiatric Service Dogs. If you get a dog that is a retired show dog, you will have found a dog that is used to crowds and other animals. This means that the outside world will not be distracting to them. But this also means that as an adult, they may have experienced situations in their lives that can create triggers or difficulties. This can make it harder for them to be trained, especially if they were traumatized at an early age by people or animals. Sometimes, the dog may be startled by someone coming up behind them and smacking them on the butt, this happens often. This can create a problem, especially if the dog bites the child due to the past trauma. In the same instance, the dog could have had some negative experiences with men in hats and may respond in a negative way to a man in a hat. They may never learn how to be comfortable with those men. This can make it difficult to find a suitable adult dog that is a viable choice for your Psychiatric Service dog needs.

*No copyright infringement intended

Another concern is the lifespan of the dog that you chose. That is why you should only start with a dog that is less than or no older than 2 years old.

There are several ways to test and see which dog is best for your needs. One way is to test their temperament. By testing the temperament of the dog, you are able to find out if the dog will be able to handle tricky situations. A great test to use for this type of testing is the Volhard Temperament Test.

Consider that an adult dog has a stable temperament when living in a stable home. An adult dog that is living in the shelter will be nervous and stressed. Therefore, the temperament of that dog is going to be hard to read at first. If the puppy has its temperament at 8 weeks, this cannot viably identify the temperament of the dog. The only thing that would be reliable would be the fear and confidence levels that are exhibited in new situations. Testing the mom of a puppy can give you the highest predictor of the puppy's ability to be a Psychiatric service dog. If the mom is a competent Psychiatric Service dog with a great temperament, then the puppy will have a higher chance of being a great Psychiatric Service dog.

Due to all of this information, you should choose a pup that has a mother who is even and stable-tempered and is an acceptable Psychiatric Service dog or chose one that is living in a stable home with the right temperament. To find a puppy that is going to be the right temperament, you should find a Psychiatric Service dog breeder. The breeder can not only show you the temperament of the mother and father but also provide a family genetics of the pup. This will help you rule out any types of predispositions for genetic markers of disease and ailments. The mother is not required to be a Psychiatric Service dog for her to have a great temperament. Consider looking at dogs that are therapy dogs, dogs that have a competency in obedience or service work, as well as extremely laid-back dispositions. Many of the dogs that are being bred for show-dogs are also being bred for the proper temperament for Psychiatric Service Dogs as well.

*No copyright infringement intended

If you are interested in getting a suitable adult dog, then check into retired show-dogs. You will need a dog that has been living in a stable environment for an extended period of time. If you contact a breeder, you may be able to get a discount on a dog that has been returned or retired from being a show dog. When purchasing a dog that has been returned to the breeder, you are able to get one that is slightly cheaper as well as has a family history. Retired show-dogs have been extremely socialized. They are also trained by handlers that are experienced and knowledgeable.

The basic thing that you need to remember is that no matter which one you choose, whether breeder, rescue, pup or adult, you need to not worry about the cost of the dog since it will average out to be a great investment over the over-all lifetime of the dog. The cost of the medical care or time that is wasted on a dog that unsuitable is far more important in the long run. Since the breeder puppy can cost $2000, and a hip replacement from an inherited hip dysplasia condition can cost twice if not more than that, you really need to consider finding a dog that has a family history along with it. A dog with emotional instabilities can cost $1000 to 2000 over the 20 private lessons that will be needed by the trainer.

So, although the puppy may be the cutest option, sometimes, it is best to go with an older dog so that you do not have to invest extra time and training into the puppy that has to obtain basic obedience, as well as potty training and chewing behaviors.

In the end, you are able to make the choice of whether you want to find your dog from the shelter or breeder and whether that dog will be a baby or an adult dog. It is all determined by how much money you want to spend in the long run over the lifetime of the dog.

*No copyright infringement intended

In the next chapter, you will learn about picking the right accessories and equipment that you will need for your Psychiatric Service Dog. I have given details about several types of collars and harnesses as well as leashes and how they benefit your training.

Chapter 4: Picking the Right Equipment for Your Dog

Once you have located the exact dog that you will be using for your Psychiatric Service, you will need to determine what equipment as well as collars and leashes you will want to use. There are several options on the market today and determining what you will use is based on your preference and needs.

A collar or harness has always been debated about within the dog owner's community. Several people believe strongly that a collar can cause choking and they are right, however, your Psychiatric Service Dog should never be in a position that it would be choked by its collar. Many people believe that harnesses are the best for training and walking your dog. They feel that since it does not attach to the throat area, then it adds a safer way of keeping your dog under control. In this chapter, I will discuss the differences between the two and what you should consider making the deciding factor.

*No copyright infringement intended

Collar vs. harness

What is the difference between a collar and a harness? Which one is the best for your dog? Which one will help you with the training process for a Psychiatric Service Dog? What will help you with your needs?

These are all questions that should be asked to help determine which one will provide you with the best options. There are some advantages to each one and I will list below the different advantages.

- A harness is good for using when training a puppy that has not fully learned to walk. The harness can prevent the dog from getting tangled with the leash as well as hurting themselves.

- Harnesses provide more control for the handler. This is extremely important for when training your dog on a busy street or large crowded area.

- When training an exceptionally large dog, you are able to have more control. This will also provide you that ability to take it easy on your back and arms.

- If a small dog pulls or tugs on a leash, they will be more easily able to get injured. Since the harness can help the pressure from the leash to be dispersed throughout the dog's body, this will lower the strain that is caused on the dog's back as well as the neck.

- A harness will also discourage the dogs from pulling. The harness can be attached to the dog's chest or shoulder blades. This will redirect the dog to not pull anymore since the pulling will not get him any results.

- Harnesses also provide a way for the dog to be confined to the leash without having the ability to escape the leash. Many dogs are little escape artists and they will wiggle out of their collars and take off, when not professionally trained. The harness prevents this from happening.

A few more pros about harnesses are listed below:

*No copyright infringement intended

• They are an effective tool for training. This is especially true for puppies.

• Harness work well for most breeds but specific breeds are highly benefited by wearing a harness. These dogs include pugs that are prone to having their eyeballs popping out due to pressure around their neck.

• They help you provide a more controlled pressure for the dog which discourages them from pulling or tugging on the handler, as well as jumping.

• They will keep a distracted pup to focus extremely.

• A dog with a short nose is also a great candidate for using a harness. This is another reason a pug should be harnessed.

• If the dog has a neck injury or respiratory issues, then a harness will help with this. Due to the stress that a collar places on the throat when tugged, the windpipe can be aggravated, and this will cause coughing.

However, there are a few cons to using a harness. These will be listed below.

• Your dog may not be particularly fond of the harness.

• A harness that is clipped at the back will not be a complete success for your dog. The back-clip harnesses train the dog to focus their attention away from the handler which is not a good thing.

Now, I will discuss the benefits of a collar for a dog in training. Below are the pros that can be derived about a collar when used for your dog in training.

• The can be a clever idea for the pups that dislike the harness and need that extra comfort.

- They are visible and function properly. They are able to provide a spot for your dog's identification, rabies tags, and license tag. This makes them convenient.

However, there are many cons about collars and your dogs. These can be located below.

*No copyright infringement intended

- They do not provide ideal training tools.

- If the dog pulls slightly then it can increase the chances of an injury to the neck.

- The collar can cause pressure on the eye when they pull, and this can worsen the dog's progression of glaucoma or even increase signs of eye injuries.

- They can also increase the chances of thyroid problems as well as behavioral problems because of the increased pain and injuries to the ears and eyes due to the pressure on the neck.

As a precaution, a collar should be worn for identification purposes and harnesses for training and walking.

There are several varieties of harnesses and collars that can be purchased, each with a unique style and function. Below is a breakdown of the style of collars and harnesses that I have used in the past or have researched.

Flat Buckle Collar

The flat buckle collar is a popular one that many people use. This is mainly because it is basic and widely found. These are great for identification purposes. However, they do allow for the dog to pull and cause neck strain. If your dog is well-trained to walk on a leash and does not pull out of their collar, then this will do nicely.

Body Harness

Body harnesses are another extremely popular harness that is applied with a back attachment and is used most often with the small dog breeds. This harness is designed to prevent the throat from being damaged when the dog pulls on the leash. It also is quite helpful in keeping the leash from getting tangled underneath the dog's legs. The body harness will offer more control to the handler and less the control to the dog. This will require you to have more control and strength. If you want to allow your dog to run and exercise, then the longer leash is ideal for this type of harness.

Easy Walk Harness

Easy Walk Harness has a leash attachment with a front facing harness. This can redirect the dog's attention away from pulling and also allow the handler to pull them back. The flexibility of the harness is a wonderful way to protect your dog that is sensitivities to the neck and it allows you to have 4 different adjustment points that can be a perfect fit for your dog.

Soft Mesh Harness

Soft mesh harnesses are another wonderful way to get a fashionable harness for your pet. They are lightweight and provide a breathable harness for the dog. With the quick release style buckle, you can easily adjust the harness. They come in eight different brightly colored hues. These are a great option for small dogs especially the toy breeds. They are also a broad selection for dogs that are sensitive around the neck and puppies that need softer harnesses.

Nylon Dog Harness

Nylon dog harnesses is a simple to adjust harness made of nylon that can come in several sizes with fun colors to suit an individual's personality. They can be priced very reasonably and suitable for all dogs.

Cooling and Reflective Harness

Harnesses with a cooling and reflective feature are another great option. They provide a cooling effect with a reflective quality. The cooling harness has a cooling pack that can be replaced for keeping the dog cool in the hotter months. Fill your pockets with some chilly water and place in the freezer and this is guaranteed to keep the dog cool while doing agility and also hiking or hot weather walking.

*No copyright infringement intended

Front Hook Harness

Front hook harness looks similar to the body harness listed above except the leash is attached in a different position which is on the front of the dog's chest area. This is a great harness for walking your dog since if the dog pulls, the harness will apply leverage and keep them from pulling.

Head Halters

Halters for the head are another way to apply a halter to your dog for control. This will provide you with all the control for your dogs head and it keeps the dog in check and under control. This will give you the most opportunity for control when walking your dog. If you have an exceptionally large dog, then this is a great harness for you to use. It also provides leverage which allows you to use less strength for the control. Using a long leash should never be done with a head halter. This can injure the dog if he pulls and is suddenly stopped by the leash.

Martingale Collars

Martingale collars are another collar that many people have been using lately. Because of its ability to tighten around the neck of the dog, it has limited opportunity to slip off the dog's neck. The tightening only goes as far as the adjustment on the collar will allow. The traditional choke chain can cause lots of damage to the neck, so this collar was designed to not do the damage that the choke chain would do. However, it still provides the same function. Since dogs will wiggle out of their collars, this collar was designed to prevent that from happening. The leash is attached to a loop that is located on the collar and this helps the collar tighten when needed.

Leashes and the variety that you can choose from

Leashes are another accessory that is needed for training a dog for Psychiatric Services. Leashes come in several lengths as well as several styles. The leash that you chose is the most important piece of equipment for training your dog. A leash provides the handler with control as well as enforces the training procedures. By using the appropriate leash, this will help the dog to learn what is and is not an acceptable behavior. In about every state, there is a leash law that states that a leash is required for pets and service animals. Leashes help to train your dog how to behave properly. They also allow you to keep your dog safe and secure when outside.

Below, I have listed some of the most popular leashes on the market and then I will go into a bit of detail about how they can help you with your needs.

- The Martingale leashes

- The Standard flat lead

- The Slip Leads

- The bungee and Stretchable rubber leashes

- The Retractable leashes

- The Gentle leader headcollar

- The Harness leads

The Martingale Leashes

The Martingale leash is similar in style to the Slip lead since they both function as a collar and a lead. This lead looks like a collar that is attached to a lead adding adjustability to the lead. This was designed for a smaller head and a thicker neck such as Greyhounds. This means that it prevents the dog from backing out of the collar instead of being able to. It tightens on the dog to stop this behavior. These are not seen very often among dog trainers but can be used successfully with dogs that are prone to pulling. The martingale tightens to the strength at which it is being pulled. This leash also has an easy to attach and detach collar and leash. This means that it takes no time to put the lead on and off, so using it for a quick lead is a great idea.

*No copyright infringement intended

The Standard Flat Lead

This is the standard leash that everyone is using. They have a simple clamp or clasp that helps attach the leash to the collar or harness that is on the dog. They come in 4 foot or 8-foot lengths. They will clip onto the collar and allow your dog to have a range of walking space. The material options for a flat lead can be anything from nylon to leather. There are several styles and the most popular ones are the ones that have a rope-like appearance. Since they are excellent quality and strong, they can work with any dog. They will provide a good bit of safety and allow the handler to have control of the dog. It is best to start off with a 4-foot leash so that you can be sure to have all the control. Once the dog is used to the procedures and has all the training they need, you can then extend your leash to a longer length. This is a staple in the accessories department of having a dog even a Psychiatric Service Dog.

The Slip Leads

This is the leash style that is used at shelters. They function as both a collar and a leash. They are often used for training dogs since they are easily attached and detached from the dog's neck. They will look as if they are a regular leash, but they will have a small metal ring at the end of the leash. By pulling the leash through the metal ring, you can create a sort of collar to wrap around the dog's neck, creating a seamless leash and collar. The placement of this leash on a dog is especially important. It should be high up on the dog's neck closer to the ears so that it will not cause the dog to have any throat issues such as coughing or choking. This can be a sensitive area to the dog, so it will prevent the dog from pulling hard on the leash. This is not a long-term solution for dog training or safety.

*No copyright infringement intended

The Bungee and Stretchable Rubber Leashes

This is a leash that should be avoided at all costs. This does not provide a proper control for the handler when trying to correct the dog's behaviors. Since the bungee or stretchable lead is going to bounce back itself, this means that the handler is not getting all the control they need to train the dog. This will negate the ability of the handler to manage the dog.

The Retractable Leashes

A retractable leash is able to provide your dog up to 30 feet of leash freedom. The leash is a thin braided rope that comes out of a plastic handle. The handle contains a mechanical system that will allow the leash to extend to full length as well as a button that helps you retract the leash with a simple push of the button. It also provides a way to stop the leash from extending and retracting any further than a certain point. It is an extremely ineffective leash when needing a controlled environment. Since this does not have a quick response time, it allows the dog to get too far away and not provide enough control for the handler. This can lead to situations that can get extremely dangerous, especially if another dog confronts the dog. Another thing that is not effective with this leash is that the thin braided rope can get tangled up inside the mechanisms and be useless. It can also tangle up around the dog's legs and other extremities, as well as the hands of the owner. By using a retractable leash, you can influence your dog to believe that they are in control of you instead of you being in control of them. This does not give the dog clear boundaries and can be confusing to them.

*No copyright infringement intended

The Gentle Leader Headcollar

This is similar to a horses muzzle and provides a gentler way to stop the pulling. This harness is slipped over the nose of the dog and used to pull the dog back to you with a gentle tug of the head towards you. This will redirect the dog's attention and give them a clear sign of who is in control. This, however, is an extremely uncomfortable leash for the dog. The dog's body language will give you a clue into how they feel about this type of harness and leash. If the dog shows signs of not liking it, then I would suggest not using it. The leash can cause hair loss around the muzzle as well as permanent indentions that can be uncomfortable for the dog. If you want a professionally trained dog, then this leash is not a great option since it just teaches them that you will jerk their head in the instance that they pull.

The Harness Leads

This is a lead and a harness that comes in one piece. This is usually used for dogs that jump. It is an effective way to teach them not to jump. The harness lead can tighten up around the dog's body when he tries to jump or pull. This harness will lessen the pressure that is applied to the trachea, and this is always a great option. However, making sure you use it properly is necessary to avoid the misuse of the leash and avoid the injuries that could ensue. On the other hand, using a traditional harness can provide too much pressure on the chest area, and this will result in the dog pulling much harder on the leash.

*No copyright infringement intended

So, which leash is best for what type of dog and what should you chose seems to be the main question when it comes to leashes and your new Psychiatric Service Dog. If you have a hyper dog, you will need a leash that will allow you to control the dog. If the dog is not very hyper and tends to be laid back, then a leash that is looser in control will be a fine option for this type of dog. Every dog is different, and every leash provides a different amount of control as well as functionality.

Simple leash and collar

A simple leash with a collar can be an excellent choice for keeping a dog balanced and safe by your side. However, this is only best for the happy-go-lucky and calm dog. A dog with proper obedience training can be quite easily controlled with this leash.

Slip collar

If your dog presents issues while on a walk, a training lead can provide a great a tool which offers a huge amount of control when the dog is misbehaving. This is a great collar and leash for a dog that gets easily distracted and can be a great asset for getting your dog's attention back to the task at hand. By giving a firm pull that is quick and to the side, you can divert the dog's attention back to the handler. This will knock the dog off balance and redirect his attention to the handler instead of the act of pulling. This will also allow you to keep the safety of your dog in mind, allowing you to give a safe correction to the dog.

Chapter 5: Pet Insurance and Caring For Your Psychiatric Service Dog

*No copyright infringement intended

Another thing you will need to research as well as consider when looking to obtain or train your own Psychiatric Service Dog is the pet insurance and the amount of responsibility that you will have when caring for your dog.

Pet insurance is something that can be provided by a few service companies. There are also payment programs within veterinarian offices that provide you veterinarian services on a monthly payment basis. This is not a payment plan for services rendered, but a plan that charges you per month for services yet to be rendered.

In this chapter, we will break down the benefits and advantages of owning a pet insurance plan and the specific types that are available. I will also discuss the necessary services that your Psychiatric Service Dog will need to be fit as a fiddle. Then lastly, I will talk about how a wellness plan can differ from a pet insurance plan and what benefits you get from using one.

Pet Insurance vs. Wellness Plans with the Vet

Pet insurance is not like a traditional insurance plan for humans. If I was to go out and purchase an insurance plan for myself, it would cover routine check-ups and have a small coverage plan for the emergency services and surgeries. However, with a pet insurance plan, you will need to be covered for the check-ups in some other way since the insurance plan only covers the emergency services and illnesses that suddenly arise. These are services that could have potentially broken the handler's saving bank account. The pet wellness plan is what would be needed to simply cover the routine check-ups.

*No copyright infringement intended

So, what do you get with a pet insurance plan?

With insurance coverage, you get several coverage benefits. Many of these covered services can be quite expensive without an insurance plan and although we all think this will never happen to us, it usually does.

With an insurance plan, you will have coverage for:

- Surgery
- Illness
- Accidents
- Orthopedic conditions
- Emergency care
- Therapy
- Hereditary and congenital conditions
- Prescription medication
- X-rays
- MRI's
- Hospitalization
- Cat Scans
- Ultrasounds, etc.

What do you get with a Wellness Plan?

With a wellness plan, you get coverage for all those things that are not covered by a traditional pet insurance plan. This can include several benefits that will last you for years to come since your dog will need many rounds of shots and check-ups.

The coverage options you will receive when purchasing a pet wellness plan is listed below:

- Teeth Cleanings
- Annual Exams

- Urinalyses

- Spay/neuter

- Flea, tick and heartworm treatments

- Routine vaccinations (rabies, DHLP, Bordetella, Parvo, Lyme, giardia)

- Routine blood panels

- Heartworm testing

- Microchip

- Fecal testing

With pet insurance, oftentimes, you are able to include a wellness plan as an add-on. However, not all insurance plans offer this wellness plan as an add-on. Several of the options that you have for purchasing a pet insurance plan and a wellness add-on plan will be discussed in detail below, so you can see the benefits that each one will offer your Psychiatric Service Dog.

*No copyright infringement intended

PetsBest Routine Care Coverage with Wellness Plans

Pets Best Routine Care Coverage Plan is one of the most popular options. They have two coverage options for the wellness plan. These are:

- BestWellness

- EssentialWellness

These are additional products that can be added to the insurance plan that you purchase for your pet. Each one covers many different treatments and services. Although they cover these wellness services, there is a per item limit that must be understood. You must also add your wellness package within 30 days of purchasing the pet insurance plan, as well as within 30 days of the insurance plans renewal. The coverage costs anywhere from $14-30 per month, and this depends on the type of plan you choose to purchase for your pet, as well as whatever state you live in. It also has a rating or cap per item, which means the wellness plan will only cover the vaccinations for $80 and the annual exam at $50. If your veterinarian charges more, you would need to cover the difference.

With this plan you will have no deductibles for services rendered and your coverage will begin the day after you pay.

*No copyright infringement intended

The breakdown for PetsBest can be seen in this friendly little chart.

	EssentialWellness	BestWellness
Per month	$16 for every state but Washington where it is $14	$26 in every state but Washington where it is $30
Spay/neuter-teeth	$0	$150

whitening		
Rabies	$15	$15
Flea/tick prevention	$50	$65
Heartworm Prevention	$30	$30
Vaccination/titer	$30	$40
Wellness exam	$50	$50
Heartworm test with FELV screen	$25	$30
Blood, Fecal, Parasite Exam	$50	$70
Microchip	$20	$40
Urinalysis or ERD	$15	$25
Deworming	$20	$20
Total Annual Benefits	$305	$535

24PetWatch Wellness Coverage with Wellness Plans and Advanced Wellness Plans

This insurance plan has 2 additional coverage options for a wellness plan. Each one of these plans will have limits to what it covers. These plans start at $10 per month for the routine wellness add-on and the $25 per month advanced wellness coverage. With this plan, there is no deductible. I have included a chart below for you to see the differences in coverage. This will help you see the differences between two diverse types of coverage options between the two companies.

	Routine Wellness	Advanced Wellness
Dental Cleaning	N/A	$100
Fecal screen		

Heartworm/flea prevention	N/A	$55
Heartworm test or FELV screen	$15	$15
Microchip procedure and or urinalysis	$20	$20
Spay/neuter procedure and or wellness blood test	$80	$100
Wellness exam	$40	$50
Canine Bordetella vaccine/titer or feline FELV vaccine/titer	N/A	$15
Canine DHLPP vaccine/titer or Feline FVRCP vaccine/titer	$15	$15
Rabies vaccine/titer and/or Lyme vaccine/titer, or FIP vaccine/titer	$15	$15

ASPCA Pet Health Insurance with a Preventative Plan

The ASPCA offers 2 separate preventative plans that cover the routine services that are used to keep your Psychiatric Service Dog from getting ill. This is a basic plan that has limited services compared to a prime plan that has more services provided outside of the ones offered by the basic plan. These preventative plans will be covered under the Hartville brand. With the preventative plan, there is no waiting period as well as no deductible.

Below is a chart to help you understand the coverages that are available to you through this plan.

	Basic	Prime
Per month	$9.95	$24.95
Dental cleaning	$100	$175
Rabies or Lyme vaccination/titer	$20	$25
Flea/heartworm prevention	$0	$50
DHLP vaccine/titer	$20	$25
Bordetella vaccine/titer	$0	$25
Fecal Test	$20	$25
Wellness exam	$50	$50
Heartworm test	$20	$25
Blood test	$0	$25
Microchip	$20	$40

Urinalysis	$0	$25
Health Certificate	$0	$25
Deworming	$20	$25
Total Annual Benefits	$250	$500

As you can see, each one offers two different purchase options for the wellness add-on with an insurance plan. Each one has a set amount of coverage and provides you with several preventive measures or testing options. With stand-alone insurance, this only covers a few emergency situations and illnesses that arise when they are unexpected.

The benefits that are offered for a wellness plan can include several of these options.

- Wellness exams
- Microchipping
- Grooming
- Deworming
- Parasite prevention
- Vaccinations
- Behavior training
- Dental care
- Spaying/Neutering
- Routine screenings

And when combined with an insurance pet plan, you can gain added benefits that will help in those times of emergency need. These benefits include the ones listed below.

- Accidents
- Orthopedic conditions
- Hereditary and congenital conditions
- Illnesses
- Prescription medications

- Emergency care

When you sign up for a wellness plan, you are able to only pay for what you use, and it is covered by a small monthly payment. With insurance, you will pay a monthly fee that will provide you coverage with an annual limit, a per-incident deductible, and a reimbursement rate with no routine care. This will determine how much your monthly cost will be based on the percentages or limit that you have for services per year.

Below is an example of what you can expect when signing up for the insurance policy for your pet.

*No copyright infringement intended

PetFirst Insurance

Annual limit	$10,000
Per incident deductible	$250
Reimbursement rate	80%
Routine care	N/A
Monthly rate	$80.50

Annual limit	$10,000

Per incident deductible	$250
Reimbursement rate	80%
Routine care	$250
Monthly rate	$97.50

PetPlan

Annual limit	$10,000
Per incident deductible	$100
Reimbursement rate	90%
Routine care	N/A, lab tests, dietary supplements, End of life euthanasia,
Monthly rate	$50.72

Embrace

Annual limit	$15,000
Per incident deductible	$750
Reimbursement rate	80%
Routine care	N/A, wellness coverage $250, lab $10,000, dietary supplements $250 as part of the wellness plan, End of life and burial $10,000, $250, end of life euthanasia $10,000, Travel coverage $10,000 injuries and illness only.
Monthly rate	$21.02

Trupanion

Annual limit	unlimited
Per incident deductible	$250 per condition
Reimbursement rate	90%
Routine care	N/A, lab-unlimited, dietary supplements-unlimited, End of life

	and burial-unlimited, end of life euthanasia-unlimited, Travel coverage-unlimited-injuries and illness only.
Monthly rate	$35.04

ASPCA

Annual limit	$2,500 lifetime annual limit
Per incident deductible	$250
Reimbursement rate	70%
Routine care	$2500-unlimited with additional preventative care, travel coverage without home visit inside the US and Canada
Monthly rate	$12.89

Each one of these companies has a different standard for which they base their coverage on and each one of these rates is being shown with various levels of coverage. This is to give you a basis with which you can apply for coverage. We all have varying needs and income levels, as well as dogs. These rates are based on a younger dog, an Australian Shepherd, with no pre-existing conditions or genetic markers.

As you can see, you are able to opt for an insurance plan that is a stand-alone policy, or you can opt into an insurance plan and wellness package. If you are not concerned about injuries or accidents happening with your dog, then a wellness stand alone is another option that may be the right choice for you. Whatever you choose is based on your needs, your financial abilities, and your availability within your area.

Chapter 6: Government Regulations

*No copyright infringement intended

Since the government has a hand in all things within the US, I will go over a few of the regulations that are the deciding factors you need to consider when training your own Psychiatric Service Dog. The Americans with Disabilities Act has specific coverage that pertains to the laws about individuals with disabilities, housing, public access spaces, traveling, and much more. They also help to identify what a person with disabilities or impairment is and how to acknowledge the Psychiatric Service dogs that are cared for by those that are disabled and their rights as disabled individuals. The ADA states that disabled and impaired individuals who have a Psychiatric Service dog will need to have access to their Psychiatric Service dog at all times, and thus are allowed to bring them to the doctors, hospital, on a plane, train, bus or any other public access facility or transport. It also states that housing has to make a reasonable accommodation for the person that is disabled to live with their service animal.

How Do I Register My Psychiatric Service Dog?

In order to have a Psychiatric Service Dog, it needs to be trained properly. As per the laws under the ADA, you do not have to pay someone to train your dog for the services that you need. However, it does need to provide an actual service outside of making you feel emotionally better. The diverse types of tasks that your dog can perform for you are based on your Psychiatric needs. The Psychiatric Service dog needs to provide a service for the disabled individual based on their disability. These tasks can include:

- Redirecting or interrupting a compulsive behavior that is destructive.

- Locating something that the disabled person may need or helping them find a safe place when disoriented in a large crowd.

- Searching through a room for someone that struggles with PTSD.

- Providing guidance for the handler who suffers from dissociative disorders.

- Alertness to sounds that can be alarming for the handler or to smoke as well as security alarms when they sound off.

- Aid with balance for a handler in need of security and walking support.

- Locate and bring medication or other objects to the handler at the times that it is needed.

The next step once your dog is trained for the specific service that you will need is to make the decision on whether or not you want to register the Psychiatric Service Dog for a Psychiatric Service dog registration organizations certificate. Registering is not a necessary step since it is not a legal requirement. The benefit to registering is that they can provide you with an identification card for your dog, as well as vests, ID badges, and a certificate that shows they are a registered Psychiatric Service Dog. These things will be particularly useful when you head out into the world with a Psychiatric Service Dog, especially a vest. Often times, you will be asked if the dog is a Psychiatric Service dog and sometimes they even ask for proof, although it is very illegal for them to do so. If you decide to go this route, make sure the company you register with is a reputable company. This will ensure that the certification is legitimate.

*No copyright infringement intended

The ADA for Owners of People with Psychiatric Service Dogs Owners

Under the ADA, only dogs are recognized as Psychiatric Service animals. This means that as a Psychiatric Service dog, they are acknowledged under the ADA laws and standards. These standards have been set in place for a number of years. The definition of a Psychiatric Service dog is a dog that is trained to perform a specific task that is useful to the disabled individual's disability. This dog should be able to perform specific tasks as well as perform work that relates to the disabled person. Any public access building or facility must allow the Psychiatric Service dog to accompany the disabled individual in all areas that the public or a member is allowed to go.

Service animals qualify as working animals not pets and the tasks must be causally related to the disabled person's disability. If the dog is only providing comfort or emotional support, then they do not qualify as a service animal under the ADA. However, they do fall under the Emotional Support Animals Standard that is set by the Housing Authority. Although this definition for service animal can be limiting, it does not affect the broader definition of assistance animal that is described under the Air Carrier Access Act.

There are several states and local laws that provide a broader definition than the ADA would provide. This information is found through the states' Attorney General Office.

Where can I take my Service Animal?

Due to the laws that are set by the ADA, your local and state government and several nonprofit organizations that provide services for the public have to allow a service animal within their facility to accompany the disabled individual. These accesses only apply to the areas that the public has normal access to. A service animal can enter a hospital with a patient that is disabled, as well as cafeterias, examination rooms, and even ER's. However, if the entry of a service animal would cause issues for the area or people within the area, then the service animal can be excluded. These include operating rooms or burn units since the presence of the service animal could create an unsterile environment.

What can exclude an individual service animal from having access?

The service animal must be under the handlers complete control at all times while in the building. They must be harnessed, leashed or tethered unless the use of these accessories would hinder the service animal's service work for the individual, or the disability prevented the use of these accessories. If this is the case, the disabled person has to have complete control of the animal by voice or signal command.

If the service the dog is performing for the disabled person is not readily obvious to the business owner, then they are allowed to ask a limited amount of questions to ascertain that the dog is a service animal. They may only ask two questions to the disabled person about the service animal.

- Is this service animal required due to a disability?

- What task is the service animal providing for the disabled person?

The staff is not allowed to ask any questions about the disability of the person, nor ask for medical documentation. They cannot require an ID for the dog or any type of training certificate. They cannot ask for the dog to demonstrate its ability to do its task or be shown the task that it performs.

The fear of a dog is not a valid excuse to exclude the service animal from entry. It can also not be excluded from allergies. If there is a person in the same classroom or homeless shelter with someone that has an allergy to dogs or pet dander, then an accommodation has to be made for each person to be comfortable. They must be provided a separate space to sit in or sleep in if there is a possibility for this.

Those with a disability cannot be asked or forced to remove a Psychiatric Service dog from the property of a business or public access facility unless these two things happen.

- The dog becomes out of control and the handler cannot handle them.

- The dog is not potty trained.

If this takes place, then they have to offer the individual with the service animal the opportunity to purchase the things they need with the presence of the service animal.

If the establishment sells food or prepares food, then they have to provide the service animal the right to enter public areas, even if the local or state health codes prohibit the entry of animals within the area.

A disabled person that is using a service animal cannot be separated from the other people within a facility or business due to the service animal and cannot be charged extra fees for that service animal. If the business requires deposits for guests with pets, this fee must be waived for the service animal.

If a hotel charges guests for damage from themselves or their pets, they are allowed to charge for anything damaged by the guest or the Psychiatric Service dog.

The staff within a hotel or business is not required to provide any services or food to the service animal. Nor are they required to provide care for the service animal.

Although this book is about a Psychiatric Service Dog, there are a few laws that provide Miniature Horses a few rights under the ADA laws. If the Miniature Horse provides a service or performs tasks for a disabled person, they fall within the guidelines of a service animal. This is further defined by what a Miniature Horse would be. They are 24 inches up to 34 inches tall when measured from the bottom of the hoof to the top of the shoulders. They also must weigh between 70-100 pounds. If the disabled person is using a Miniature Horse as a service animal, then they must be provided reasonable accommodations. There are 4 ways to assess the Miniature Horse to determine the accommodation within the facility.

- Is the Miniature Horse potty trained?

- Is the Miniature Horse under the handler's control?

- Does the facility have space to accommodate the Miniature Horse's size, type, weight, and such?

- Will the presence of the Miniature Horse compromise the safety requirements that legitimately provide a safe operational facility?

Housing Authority for Owners of Psychiatric Service Dog Owners

Under the 504 that is outlined in the Rehabilitation Act of 1973 within the Americans with Disabilities Act, they define service animals as animals that aid those that are disabled. However, the Department of Justice limits this definition to only dogs and then excludes emotional support animals from being defined as a service animal. Under the Housing Authorities, emotional support animals are covered for reasonable accommodations as an assistance animal. What this means is that a person with a disability can expect reasonable accommodations when renting a place and having a service animal or emotional support animal. The FHA and the ADA cover housing that is public, or ran by a leasing office, or real estate office, as well as housing for universities.

Title II law applies to housing that is public entities, as well as government housing and universities. Title III applies to rental offices and shelters, along with multifamily dwellings, facilities that provide assisted living, and public education housing. The 504 also provides covers for those houses that receive financial assistance for their housing needs. HUD covers all types of housing. This will include privately owned and federal assisted houses. However, there are some limited exclusions that are exceptions to the rules. In housing situations where there is a no pets rule, the property owner must allow and provide reasonable accommodations for disabled individuals who have or wish to have a service animal. Since an assistance animal is not a pet, the no pet policy, pet deposit, or pet rent does not apply to these animals. The definition of a service animal has been described throughout this book several times, and it pertains to this definition as well.

For reasonable accommodations, there is no governing law that requires the dog to be individually trained by a specific program or certified or registered under any specific organization. Dogs are the only one covered as service animals. However, an emotional support animal is an animal that provides emotional support to the individual. If the request is submitted for a resident to use an assistance animal, then they must follow the general principles that are applicable for the accommodations that have been requested. They must then consider these things to assess the accommodation.

- Does this person have a disability?

- Does this disabled person have a service animal that provides a service for their disability? Or emotional support which helps with the alleviation of the person's disability symptoms?

If the answer is no to either one of these, then the accommodation is not required, and the request could be denied. If the answer to each question is yes, then the accommodation must be made. The only exclusion is if the accommodation would create undue financial burdens or alter the fundamental nature of the said property.

For instance, if the service animal has shown that they are a direct threat to others' safety and cannot be changed by another accommodation, then they can be denied, or in the case where the specific animal in question would cause damage to the property that cannot be eliminated or avoided by another accommodation.

This cannot be based on the size of the dog, the breed, or the weight. And to deny the animal the decision must be based on that individual animal and not a generalized fear or speculation. Nor can it be based on a previous service animal or dog in the past.

The restrictions or conditions that are applied to pets within housing communities cannot be imposed on a service animal. For instance, the pet deposit does not apply to a service animal or emotional support animal, nor does the monthly rent. Denial cannot take place based on the housing owner's uncertainty about the person's disability or need for a service animal's services. If the disability is not apparent, they can ask for reliable documentation that is provided by a physician, psychiatrist, social worker, or other mental health professionals to explain the need for the service animal. This will provide enough documentation. The letter does not have to be specific about the disabilities of the patient.

They cannot, however, ask for the person to submit medical records or provide them access to the provider of their medical needs. They also cannot request them to provide details as well as extensive material evidence about their disability with documentation from a clinical examination. Each reasonable accommodation request is individually assessed for each person. They cannot conditionally deny the accommodation or charge a fee such as a deposit as terms for the applicant's service animal to be allowed. They also cannot delay the response for an unreasonable amount of time.

If you find that you are denied unfairly, then contact the HLTD to file a complaint about the denial.

Although emotional support animals are covered under the HUD guidelines, they are not considered service animals. They simply provide emotional support, comfort, companionship, and well-being support for the disabled individual. Because of the definition of a service animal, only a dog as well as a Miniature Horse can be considered a service animal under the ADA.

With this said, I will proceed to the next chapter where I will start to give in-depth details about how to train your Psychiatric Service Dog for the specific services that you need.

*No copyright infringement intended

Chapter 7: Public Access Requirements for a Psychiatric Service Dog

What they need to know to enter buildings, fly on planes, and such

Public Access Skills

As an owner of a Psychiatric Service dog, you are required to train your dog to perform certain tasks, as well as make sure that they are under control at all times while out in the public. There are a few things that you will need to make sure your dog is properly trained before they are allowed to be on public transportation or out in public buildings as a Psychiatric Service dog. These things are listed below.

- Sit on command in various situations - the Psychiatric Service Dog needs to understand that when you say sit, it sits in and it stays without trying to get up and wander around.

- Controlled loading into and unloading out of a vehicle - they need to be under control while being loaded into a vehicle or unloaded from a vehicle.

- Down on command in various situations - They need to understand and respond appropriately when you tell them to lie down.

- Controlled approach to a building - They need to be completely under your control when they approach a new building or any building for that matter.

- Controlled entry and exit through a doorway - They need to be under control when entering new buildings or existing buildings that they have already visited. Doorways can be scary for a dog and entering through one is necessary for most activities.

- Control when the leash is dropped - If you happen to drop the leash, they need to be under your control and not chase after animals, people, or simply wander off.

- Control in a restaurant - They need to be able to lie underneath the table at a restaurant and not present a problem for the restaurant.

- Heeling through a building - They need to be able to heel while in a building and not create any problems.

- Six-foot recall on lead - They need to be comfortable on a six-foot recall lead and not try to pull away or cross the path of others.

*No copyright infringement intended

How they need to react with other animals and people

A service animal needs to respond to people and animals as if they are not present. Most service animals wear vests, and these vests will say that they are a service animal and ask for no one to pet them. Although this is recommended for some animals, there are sometimes when I have been able to pet a service animal. It is a good rule of thumb to ask the handler if it is ok before approaching the dog. A dog that is aggressive towards children or other people is not a proper Psychiatric Service dog.

When the Psychiatric Service dog is walking down the street, they should be completely oblivious to the other animals on the street or the other people. It should be hyper-focused on what the handler is doing and if the handler needs any help.

The next two chapters are all about the Psychiatric Service Dog training techniques for specific services that can be performed by the dogs and whom they will benefit. One of the training techniques is on retrieving and this is something that all people with disabilities can use to help them with their daily life.

Chapter 8: Step By Step Training of a Psychiatric Service Dog

Every service animal performs a specific task that is taught to them to assist you in your needs in being disabled. Although each service animal needs to have a basic obedience training course prior to being trained for service, they can actually start training for the obedience and then the service that you need them for at the same training course. You do not have to pay a trainer to train your dog for you. In fact, it is better than you train them yourself so that you are both acquainted with the training steps, and so that you can have the pack leader established.

For Anxiety and Depression Patients

A Psychiatric Service dog for Anxiety or depression will need to perform certain tasks to qualify as a Psychiatric Service Dog. These tasks can include:

- Providing comfort and support

- Collecting medication

- Using tactic stimulation to divert the handler's attention by licking the face.

- Be able to identify the signs of a panic attack or the onset of a panic attack.

- Provides a sense of purpose and job to the disabled person. Provides a reason to get out of bed or go outside. Feeding, walking, and caring for the dog.

A Psychiatric Service dog for depression is a great resource for those that struggle with leaving their homes, especially if that person is in a constant state of depression or negative thoughts, as well as when suicidal. They can help the depressed person live a fuller life.

*No copyright infringement intended

So how do you train your Psychiatric Service Dog for Depression tasks?

First, you must start with the basics. Make sure that your dog has basic obedience training such as the type you would find when signing your dog up for the Good Citizen Training.

All dogs need to have certain basic skills to begin with for being trained for their Psychiatric Service. Below are the skills that are necessary to be trained from the beginning.

- Sit and stay

- Down

- Up

- Heel

- Come

- Leave

- As well as potty outside on cue

If you are not equipped to train your dog for these simple tasks, then you will need to find a trainer that can do this for you. You should also consider paying someone to train your dog for the service that you need after the obedience is learned.

Next, you will need to determine what service the dog will be doing for you. As with most disabilities, you will need to have some way of obtaining a phone when you do not have the ability to walk or move. This is a continuing problem for those that have mobility issues as well as the elderly and those that get severely depressed. So, training your dog to retrieve is a great task for them to learn. Another task for anxiety is to identify when an anxiety attack is coming and provide tactile stimulation by licking the person or nudging the handler so that they can begin to pet the dog to reduce the anxiety and calm down quickly.

*No copyright infringement intended

Step-by-step process for training a dog to retrieve:

To do a formal retrieval, the Psychiatric Service Dog would need to be trained to take hold of an object, carry that object, and release the object into the trainer's hand. This process will take patience and determination. You will also need a profound sense of humor to accomplish this. Retrieving allows the dog to pull open doors, pick up an item that is dropped, get the phone, carry some bags, deliver a message to someone, help someone get dressed or undressed, and so much more. If you use your hands, the Psychiatric Service dog will use their mouth. It is vital that you go slow and create a pattern.

Motivational Technique for Retrieval

You can start as young as 5-7 weeks old when teaching this technique.

Start by teaching them to carry, mouth, or play with different textures. Offer them glass bottles, PVC pipe, short pieces of metal, key rings, and toys that have slick, non-fun or cool textures while supervised. If they get used to the different textures, it will be easier to teach them to retrieve objects.

*No copyright infringement intended

Prior to starting

Understand how to mark behaviors with a clicker. The timing must be impeccable, and you must be confident. This is a process that will take a long time to accomplish.

Condition the pup or adult dog by a clicker in their training

Conditioning the dog to focus on the clicker for a brief period of time and understanding the basic targeting techniques is a must.

What supplies will you need?
- Dumbbells are useful when teaching them to retrieve something. You can also use a retrieving dummy.

- Clickers

- Treats that have high value or are your dog's favorite treat. This can be things such as chicken bites, hot dogs, or other kinds of treats.

Targeting the Psychiatric Service dog

- Using a chair, sit down and have your Psychiatric Service dog face you.

- Hold out the dumbbell with the clicker.

- Place treats on the other hand.

- Show the dumbbell to your dog. Then click the clicker and place the treat in front of the nose and bump it.

- Move your dumbbell from one side to the other and continue to click the clicker while targeting the nose to bump the dumbbell and then give the dog the treat for the bump.

- Do not pay any attention to your dog's pawing or vocal commands. Only pay attention to nose bumps and then giving it the treat.

- Continue to practice these processes of targeting the dumbbell with the clicker and nose bumping, then giving the dog a treat until the dog focuses and moves a few feet in the direction of the dumbbell and nose bumps it.

Once they have targeted the dumbbell and are doing this process properly, they are ready to start mouthing the dumbbell.

*No copyright infringement intended

Mouthing the Psychiatric Service Dog

- Start by not clicking for nose bumps and just simply waiting. Do not offer leads or cues to the dog. Once the dog gets frustrated nose bumping the dumbbell without a response, it will open its mouth. Instantly click and give the dog several treats in a row. This is the response we are going for. If the dog does not touch the dumbbell that is ok, simply click, and then provide the treatment for the gaping mouth.

- Continue this process by ignoring the nose bumps but clicking and then providing a treat when the mouth opens. If he happens to brush the dumbbell with his mouth or teeth even if by accident, then click and give him a treat.

- Continue to work on this until the dog purposely opens his mouth and places it on the dumbbell, even if he instantly spits it out. Click the clicker and then give him a treat. This is training the dog mouth the dumbbell to contact.

- Once the dog has this down, start to only give the dog a treat when he does actual grabs of the dumbbell. This means that the mouth is open, and the teeth close down around it, even if for a split second. Click the clicker and then give the dog a treat.

The next part of training a Psychiatric Service dog to retrieve is teaching distance, duration, and distraction techniques. This helps increase the understanding the dog has to the behavior or command that you are cueing them for. Take each one of these, one step at a time, since they get distracted and can be confusing.

*No copyright infringement intended

At this time, the Psychiatric Service dog should be looking for a treat as soon as she hears the clicker. She should also grab the dumbbell or retrieving dummy as soon as you present it to her. Do not worry if she immediately spits it out. Your Psychiatric Service dog should also be ok with moving to the left or right a short distance to retrieve the dumbbell.

Introducing your release cue

Although it seems backward to train to release before training to hold, once they learn that they will be releasing the item into your hand, they will be able to understand that they need to wait for the cue to release it.

• Make sure that your dog can do a couple of rounds of clicking and then receiving a treat for grabbing the dumbbell. Once you get to around 3-5 reps that are quickly executed, you can move on to the next step in the process. At this point, the dumbbell should be in your hand the whole time.

• Now, you should introduce the release cue that you will be using. Present the dumbbell to the dog. Once she reaches for it and grabs it, allow her to. Then click the clicker and repeat your command for release. As she releases it to give her a treat. Continue to do this several times until the dog begins to pause, even if for just a second, prior to spitting it out. This means she is listening for the cue.

• Click the clicker for the pause between each grab and again for the release of the dumbbell. Continue to use the release command. As time progresses, you will notice a pause that builds in time. Once she starts to extend her pause, give her multiple treats, especially for lengthy pauses. Remember that the click identifies the behavior you are wishing to teach. Clicking for pause teaches them to pause. Clicking again for release and saying your release cue is teaching to release. Then give the dog treats for the clicks.

• If you can count to one Mississippi between each pause, then you are ready to move on.

Training the dog to release to your hand

Keep these sessions short. They also need to be positive and upbeat. This is going to be a frustrating session for both the handler and the dog. The goal for this session is to train the dog that they will get a reward but only if the dumbbell is placed in the handler's hands.

• Start with offering the dumbbell to the dog. When she grabs hold of it, let the dumbbell go, moving your hand underneath her chin. This is so the dog can drop the dumbbell in your hand when it lets it go. Click the clicker and give her a treat when saying your release command. If the dog releases the dumbbell prior to the release word, then move your hand out of the way and let the dumbbell fall to the ground. Do not click your clicker and do not give the dog a treat. Just look at the dog and shrug it off, pick up your dumbbell and offer it to the dog again.

• Continue this process for 5-6 times in a row.

• Do this routine over and over again. However, do not say your release word. Instead, you need to wait. If the dog drops the dumbbell again, then shrug and say nothing. Pick it up and offer it to the dog again. This time, use the release word and let the dumbbell fall into your palm. Then give your dog several treats.

- Continue to practice these steps. Every 3rd to 5th time, use the release cue randomly. However, do not use the release cue and allow the dog to spit it out. Shrug off the drop and pick up the dumbbell again and offer it to the dog. Allow the dog to grab and then use the cue to release, and let it drop in your palm. Give a treat when done properly.

- Notice when your Psychiatric Service dog purposefully holds onto the dumbbell for a longer time as if waiting for the release cue. Then use the release cue and allow it to drop properly, and then give several treats for reward.

- Continue to do this until your Psychiatric Service dog has succeeded more times than she has failed. Include the purposeful failures in order to show your dog what is not appropriate and reinforce the behavior for waiting until the release cue.

*No copyright infringement intended

Training for a guided hold

Be very gentle during this phase of training. You are using motivation to train the dog how to retrieve. You do not want to force it.

Have your dog sit beside you. Choose the opposite side of your dominant hand for your dog's position.

• Offer the dumbbell to the dog with your dominant hand. Once her teeth close on it, allow the dog and then slide your hand underneath the dog's chin.

• Stroke upwards on the dog's neck to the tip of her chin with your dominant hand. Do this for a second or two, and then stop. Next, place the dominant hand underneath to catch the dumbbell, clicking to tell the dog to hold. Then using the release cue, allow the dog to release it, and then give the dog a treat.

• Continue this process while increasing the time that the dog holds by 1-2 seconds each time, but only if the dog is calmly holding the dumbbell. If the dog is struggling, trying to spit it out, or moving around, continue to use the soft stroking technique. Take this gentle and slow. Be patient and steady with the hold. It is not a race.

• Continue to do this until the hold reaches 30 seconds with a comfortable or calm hold while stroking the chin gently.

Training the dog to hold

• Start this process as you would the guided hold. Offer the dumbbell to the dog and continue to gently stroke under the chin one to two times. Take your hand away from the chin and after a few seconds, click the clicker. Use the release cue and give the dog a treat. Once the dog releases, pet your dog calmly. If the dog does not wait for the cue to release, then simply shrug it off and pick it back up and try again.

• Repeat this process 2 or 3 more times, and then stop to stroke your dog's chin after she has taken the dumbbell. Hand it to your dog, take your hand away, and wait for 3 to 5 seconds. Use your clicker, and then cue the release. Once the dog releases it, hand her a treat.

• Over time, continue to build gradually. Gain a second or two of hold at a time. Do this until the dog can hold for at least 30 seconds until they receive the cue to release without any guidance from you.

If the dog is continuously failing at this point, then you have too many distractions or have pushed the dog to fast. Go back to the point at which the dog was succeeding and move forward from that point. Continue to be upbeat about it and set your dog up for a successful training session. If the dog continues to spit out the dumbbell, then continue the shrug and keep quiet. Pick it up and offer it to the dog again. Keep all your sessions short and to the point so the dog will not lose interest and the formal retriever training remains intact.

Train for Desensitizing Touch

At this point, your dog is used to the release cue that you chose. The dog is comfortable dropping the dumbbell into a waiting hand. Remember that this can become an issue for those dogs that start to associate touch with the release command instead of the release cue. If the handler is not ready for the item, then this becomes a problem. To counteract this, you will need to remember that giving the rewards will instill the behavior that you want to train the dog.

•	With your dog placed in front of you or on the side of you, begin to desensitize the dog to touch.

•	Hand the dumbbell to your dog, remove your hand, and then wait for a few seconds.

•	Reach up to gently touch the dumbbell's edge. If the dog drops it, then allow it to fall. Shrug and pick up the dumbbell. Then silently offer the dumbbell again. Reinforce your verbal release cue a few times, and then continue to repeat this light touch again with no cue. If your dog holds the dumbbell, immediately use the clicker and release cue, and then give the dog a reward.

•	Hand the dumbbell to the dog and stroke gently on the dogs head or its muzzle. Use the clicker and then release command. Once the dog releases, give her a treat for the continued hold and ignore all the drops entirely.

•	Continue to work with your dog until the dog waits for the release cue even if you have curled your fingers around the dumbbell. Stroke your dog's head, muzzle, ears, and touch the dumbbell to show the connection.

Train for Proofing the Hold

Once the dog has happily held the dumbbell for 30 seconds until you cue the release, then you know she has understood the training. This means that your dog understands the take and hold command. Now you need to start proof.

Proofing Game Green Eggs and Ham

This will introduce some variations of the position. Ask for the dog to take and hold while standing or sitting in front of you, as well as position on the opposite side or lying down. Next, have the dog hold it in different circumstances. For instance, standing on the stairs with you a few steps up or down the stairs or in the front seat of your car or in a kennel. Find creative ways to train for a generalized hold behavior. Are the green eggs and ham located in a box? In a car? In a house? With a mouse? Find out what places your dog will continue the take and hold training. Basically, find the wildest and craziest places that the dog will continue the performance standard.

Proofing for Movement and Positions

•   Now, you will introduce some movement into the training. Start with asking the dog to change positions while holding the dumbbell. This can start with a shift from side to side or from sitting to standing, a sit to a down, or a stand to a sit, as well as a stand to a down.

•   Ask for the dog to make one position change and then reward the dog extensively for the dog's success. Build up 3 or 5 position changes repeatedly, then ask for the release, but take it slow and gradual.

•   If the dog starts to drop the dumbbell before you ask for the cue, then you are requiring too much too fast. Go back to a point at which the dog was succeeding, then move forward much slower.

•   Once the dog can change its position without dropping the dumbbell, ask the dog to carry it while healing. Start with tiny steps and then build on 30-second intervals for heeling. Reward the dog for success and then ignore her if she drops it. Then, silently pick the dumbbell up and offer it to the dog again.

- Work on a shorter distance instead, to increase the dog's confidence level which will, in turn, help the dog succeed.

Proofing the 3 Ds

This is when you will start the 3 Ds. You have started with the duration part of the 3 Ds. The next section is the distance.

- Start with handing the dog the dumbbell, then taking a step back. Pause and then return to your dog. Using the clicker, click and then use the release cue, and offer a treat.

- Increase your distance one step at a time until you have acclimated your happy dog to be comfortable with holding the dumbbell and walking 10 steps away, turning, and then coming back to release the dumbbell.

- Once the dog is comfortable with this, increase the distractions that the dog has by adding in the public factor. Try this at a park. Ask the dog to hold the dumbbell while you prepare a meal for the dog, or while you are doing a basic obedience with a secondary dog.

- Try to be creative with the distractions, but keep your mind focused on the 3 Ds.

- Stay within close range of your dog and do not expect a long-duration for the hold, especially when introducing the distractions. Be generous with the rewards that you give the dog, and this will ensure the dog's willingness to succeed more than the dog fails. If the dog drops the dumbbell more than the dog holds it, then reduce the distractions that are around the dog and go back to a point where success was better. Gradually increase your difficulty and try again. To reduce the distractibility, move away from the stimulus and slowly move closer to gauge the dog's abilities to perform.

Train Final "Hold" Steps

At this point, your dog is taking, holding, and carrying your dumbbell. This should be a viable action in any situation with your dog. After this, you have a smooth sailing ahead.

Continue to proof the hold in all the ways you can dream of. Continue the 3 Ds and continue increasing your distance on walking away from the dog while it is holding. Always reward a job well done. Remember your cue for release, and only click when the release cue is used, and the dumbbell is returned to your hand after a verbalized cue without a simple touch or grab from the handler. Now, you need to combine the carry and distraction training while building on the distance. You are only limited with the creativity that you use to train the dog.

*no copyright infringement intended

Training To Retrieve a Specific Item or Different Items

To train your dog to retrieve added items, you will need to introduce new objects and start at the beginning. Your dog should notice after about 3-5 items, how to retrieve any object that you ask for.

There are several kits that can be used for seeding and add items in the retrieval training process.

- Water bottle

- Glass bottle

- Strips of fleece or cloth

- Metal food bowl

- Spoon

- Spare keys on a ring

- Leash

- Pen

- 12″ section of PCV/Metal Pipe

- Old Credit/ID Card

- Heavy card stock paper

- Large dumbbell

- Key fob

- Empty cans

- Cardboard squares

- Wallet

- Vest

- Small book

- Medicine bottle

- Phone

Train for Things You will Need

Using the seeding kit

You can make your own seeding kit or purchase one. This teaches them odd textures and shapes. Use up to 20 items to train your dog with a seeding kit.

Train for Assisted Pick-Up

- The point is to train the dog to gradually pick up things form a position that is difficult for you to do. So over time, get the dumbbell closer to the ground so that you can train the dog to pick things up from the ground.

- Start in a seated position, then a standing position, bent over position, sitting on the floor, or kneeling over. Whatever you need to do to get the dog to pick up from all positions is simply fine. If at some point your dog stops retrieving on cue, then start again at the last height that where the dog was successful. Then continue to move forward with the steps. Go slow and steady.

- Continue the process that you started with just lowering the dumbbell or item closer to the ground as you continue to train her to take it and hold. Hold the dumbbell as comfortable as you can while holding on. Repeat the process.

- Kneel and continue this process until the dog has this process down for every single level of retrieval. After repeating a couple of times, drop the dumbbell mid-way down your leg, and then repeat the process again.

- Go through this process for each level of retrieval. Continue to train the dog in the take and hold command until you have reached the ground. As you train the dog to retrieve it from the ground, gently remove your hand bit by bit from the dumbbell. This ensures that the dog will retrieve the dumbbell from the ground without your hand on it. Start by using your whole hand, then your palm, then your fingers, then a few fingers, then one finger and so on.

•   Lastly, place the dumbbell on the ground and place your hand close to it. Then repeat the steps as before until the dog has the concept down.

*no copyright infringement intended

Train for Shaping the Pick-Up
•   Instead of holding the dumbbell, place it at a distance from you. Sit in a chair and start the training session with the dog. Instead of speaking to the dog, gaze at the dumbbell every now and then. Once the dog starts to glance at the dumbbell, click the clicker and then offer a treat the moment the dog glances at or lowers its head towards the dumbbell.

•   Continue to shape the dog's intuition to pick up the dumbbell by a simple glance. Click the clicker and give a treat for the dog's movements that are appropriate. This can be anything from nudges, nosing, or mouthing the dumbbell.

•   Keep quiet and do not use commands or cues to help. The dog should puzzle their way to the correct answer.

•   If the dog picks it up, instantly use the clicker to click and give the dog lots of treats. If it picks it up off the ground without assistance, do the same. If it picks it up and then looks at it with a raised head, then repeat the clicker and the reward.

- Repeat these training until you place or toss the dumbbell a distance away from you and the dog goes to it, picks it up and then waits for the cue to release.

- Repeat these steps while standing, while lying down, or any other position that you may need them to retrieve something for you.

- Once the dog has this down, start using variables and repeat these steps.

Training for Proofing the Retrieve Pick Up

- When standing a distance from the object, ask the dog to retrieve it with the take it cue. If the dog responds properly, then click and reward the dog.

- Repeat this over and over again until the dog performs accurately up to 10 times without any help, do-overs, or hesitations. If this happens, then move on to another object.

- Go back to the Proofing Game Green Eggs and Ham, and train the dog for every item that you will need them to retrieve. Remember the 3 Ds and be mindful that you only train one at a time.

- This is a formal retrieve from start to finish. Celebrate and reward for this.

*no copyright infringement intended

Training for Introducing New Objects

- Start with objects that are similar in shape to the dumbbell and then change it up as the dog learns. Start with the larger items and work your way to the smaller items. Follow these steps to accomplish this for about 5 times until the dog picks up the additional items easily. Allow your dog to set their own pace and if they jump to an immediate pickup, hold and release with cue, then they have the process down.

- Start with a formal retrieval and then add in the added items. Allow the dog to sniff it and explore a bit, making sure to repeat the clicker process with these items. Start from the beginning of the process of the retrieval training for each item. Click and give treats as needed. Build up the hold time and the distance until the dog is retrieving these times on their own.

- Play the Proofing Game Green Eggs and Ham and continue to train the dog.

Train for Retrieval Seeding

Lay two to three items out with one of them being the dumbbell in a triangle-like a pattern. Leave enough space between them for your dog to easily step around them. They still need to be close to each other. Group these items so that the dog does not doubt that they relate.

Approach the triangle with the dog beside you and simply say the take cue and point towards the items. Do not specify any item, just allow him to select and pick up the object that he wants. Let the dog hold it and then use the release command. Give the dog a treat for the actions. Then repeat these steps. Continue to add items to the puzzle until you have introduced all the items to the Psychiatric Service Dog. Make sure the dog is completely comfortable with these items. Repeat the process until the dog is confident about the puzzle with up to 15 items or more. At this time, start the Proofing Game Green Eggs and Ham and work on your 3 Ds.

Psychiatric Service Dogs for Anxiety

Anxiety is a severe condition that many people suffer from. With a Psychiatric Service Dog, the anxiety sufferer can begin to live a better life. This disorder creates panic attacks, uneasiness, compulsive behaviors and such. You can train your dog to do several tasks for anxiety.

Dogs tend to have close bonds with their handlers and can be trained to identify panic attacks. This would be an individual response style training. I have listed below some steps to take to do this with your Psychiatric Service dog.

Individual Response Training
Start with a dog that has had basic obedience training and then incorporate training steps into training your dog to recognize an anxiety or panic attack.

Start by offering a treat to your dog every time you feel a panic attack coming on. This is a helpful way for the dog to identify the response and know when a panic attack is coming. Another technique to use is cuddling the animal when you feel the stress is coming on. This will help you find relief and help the animal to identify the signs. Finding the right breed is going to be important to train a dog for connecting on this level.

Remember to be patient with the training. Training a dog for public access is important and this can take up to 120 hours over a 6-month time period. Start with identifying which task the dog will need to provide. They need to identify your heart rate, muscle movements, scratching or touching of your face and other trigger spots, as well as breathing rates. Do you want your dog to lead you away? Do you want them to fetch medication? Do you want the dog to provide safety? Whatever you need to have your dog do make sure you train for that specific tasks.

*no copyright infringement intended

Anxiety alert and detection training

With this training, you will start with the same steps that you did with the previous training. However, you will be teaching them to detect anxiety alerts.

Anxiety cue with treats

- Nudge the dog's nose and reward the dog for the nudge.

- Command the dog to nudge and then add a reward for the dog's actions.

- Repeat this process until the dog has noticed the nudge.

- Change your position in order to train the dog for performing the alert in various locations and seated or standing positions. Reward the dog for each positive response.

- Decide on which anxiety cue to use to help identify the anxiety. This can be the scratching of your face or fidgeting as well as rubbing your arms.

- Provide the anxiety cue and act as if the anxiety symptom is real. Then, command the dog to nudge and reward for a positive response.

- Practice this over and over again, the same way you would the retriever process. Start to recognize when your dog identifies the anxiety cue without the command. Reward the identification instead of the command. Ignore any false alerts and shrug them off. Repeat this process several times per day for several weeks.

- As time progresses and the dog learns the trigger, remove the command altogether. Manifest an anxiety episode and leave out the command cue. Reward your dog when they respond appropriately.

- Practice in a variety of various places and positions and continue to work with your dog until they are identifying regularly.

Anxiety & Reward method for Detect Anxiety

- Identify the anxiety cue you want to use. This can be fidgeting, scratching, or any other active response.

- Use the cue in front of your dog. When the dog recognizes the cue, reward him by giving him a treat.

- Train the dog to nudge you and use a verbal cue for the command.

- Show the dog the anxiety cue and use the verbal command for the alert. When the dog starts to recognize the command and cue, reward it with a treat. When the dog does the nudge while you are experiencing the symptoms, reward your dog. Ignore any false alerts that the dog may do. Use the same training process and the retrieval training.

- Take the command away and practice using just the physical cues instead of the verbal cues. When the dog alerts to the symptoms for anxiety, then provide the dog with a reward for an appropriate response.

- Add in some complex practice time by adding a variety of circumstances that can be used within different environments with many distractions to train for the anxiety alert.

*no copyright infringement intended

Clicker Training method for Detect Anxiety

- Figure out the alert that you want to use and connect it to the nudge. If the dog nudges your hand, click the clicker and provide the dog with a treat.

- Using a verbal command that is associated with the anxiety, when the dog responds to the command, nudge the hand and then click the clicker when the dog responds properly. Give the dog a treat.

- Manifest some anxiety symptoms and use the verbal cues and physical cue to get the dogs response with a nudge. Then once the dog alerts with a nudge, click the clicker and provide a treat.

- Remove the verbal command and manifest symptoms of anxiety. Next, continue to click the clicker to show the dog that there was a positive response and provide a treat.

- Remove the clicker from the alert command and use the cue for the anxiety symptom to manifest the anxiety. When the dog responds properly, give the dog a reward for responding to the cue.

• Vary your practice in many various places, use distractions and various positions such as sitting, standing, and laying down. Continue to use step 3 if the dog is struggling with this process.

*no copyright infringement intended

For Someone with Schizophrenia

• Turning on the lights for a person with schizophrenia can be an immense help especially when they are experiencing an episode. When schizophrenics experience episodes, they can become fearful of the dark because they will see things that are not there or they will experience voices, and if they do not have lights on, they will think those voices are real.

• Start with standing next to a light switch that you want the dog to reach. Call over your dog and place him in a seated position.

• Hold out a treat on the wall about an inch above the switch. Tap the area a few times and entice the dog to leap up and push the switch with its front paws, right near the switch. If the dog succeeds, then give it a treat and praise.

• Repeat these steps above for a few times more until you think the dog has noticed the process of leaping up and touching the wall with its paws. Tap the light switch with your hand while holding the treat on the closed hand. The closed hand should be placed above the switch. Use the command that you chose for turning on/off the light. When the dog's paw has touched the light switch, give it a treat and praise. This is a transition to get the dog used to touch the light for the treat.

• Once you can get the dog to consistently touch the light when you place your hand there, you will be able to place your hand on your side and still get the dog to touch the light. Start with tapping the switch and then rewarding the action when the dog is done and sitting back down.

• Next, you will need to gradually move away from the light switch and use a command or motion to get the dog to use the action of getting the lights for you.

• This can only be used for dogs that have medium to moderate-sized build and ones that are comfortable when balancing on their hind legs. However, some of the smaller dogs are eager to jump up and turn the lights off or on. You may want to purchase a staircase for the smaller breed dogs though since they could hurt themselves by jumping high.

Schizophrenics have episodes where they see things or hear things that are not there. Here is a technique to train the dog to help with these episodes.

Dissociative disorder cue with treats

• Nudge the dog's nose and reward the dog for the nudge.

• Command the dog to nudge and then add a reward for the dog's actions.

• Repeat this process until the dog has noticed the nudge.

• Change your position in order to train the dog for performing the alert in various locations and seated or standing positions. Reward for each positive response.

• Decide on which anxiety cue to use to help identify the Dissociative disorder. This can be scratching of your face or fidgeting, as well as rubbing your arms.

• Provide the Dissociative disorder cue and Act as if the Dissociative disorder symptom is real. Then command the dog to nudge and reward for a positive response.

• Practice this over and over again the same way you would the retriever process. Then start to recognize when your dog identifies the Dissociative disorder cue without the command. Reward the identification instead of the command. Ignore any false alerts and shrug them off. Repeat this process several times per day for several weeks.

• As time progresses and the dog learns the trigger, remove the command altogether. Manifest a Dissociative disorder episode and leave out the command cue. Reward your dog when they respond appropriately.

• Practice in a variety of various places and positions and continue to work with your dog until they are identifying regularly.

Dissociative disorder is when a schizophrenic disassociates from the world around them and starts to see and hear things that do not exist. This can also allow them to manifest multiple personalities as well as have moments in their life where they are talking to other people that no one else's sees. These episodes can cause them to see aliens, bugs, people, dogs, monsters and also hear sounds that others cannot. In those moments, they can become violent, rage, aggressive, and even have been known to murder their families and even their own children. Many times, this condition needs to be hospitalized.

In the next chapter, I will continue to discuss the training techniques that can be used to train a Psychiatric Service Dog for various tasks. In this chapter, I discussed anxiety, depression, and schizophrenia. In the next chapter, I will discuss Autism, ODD, IED, and also PTSD.

Each one of the techniques that are discussed in the last two chapters can actually be incorporated for each one of these conditions. It just depends on what you need from your Psychiatric Service Dog.

Chapter 9: Step By Step Training Of A Psychiatric Service Dog Continued

For Autism/ODD/ IED

Autism is a world in which the person afflicted with it will live in and it is virtually impenetrable. Those who suffer from Autism have no idea how to connect with emotions or read social cues. They have obsessive behaviors, and it can place a strain on their family. They tend to participate in ritualistic-like behaviors that can be repetitive. This can sometimes last for hours. They tend to flap their arms, spin coins, line cars up, or filter things through their fingers. On the opposite end, they may not like to be touched or require overstimulation with touch. They tend to have higher levels of sensory receptors and these can cause overloads. They get overwhelmed and have meltdowns without a way to tell you about the problem. This can be difficult to know how to respond. However, a Psychiatric Service dog can usually help them calm down and prevent more damage when they are raging since they do not have a lot of verbal communication levels. Even the ones that can communicate still do not have the capacity to explain their emotions or what is wrong in those overwhelming moments. Loud noises as well as lights can be overwhelming to an autistic child which may cause a meltdown.

Behavior Intervention

There are several ways to help with autism, and behavior intervention is one of them. One way to provide a behavior intervention is to use a technique for interrupting repetitive behaviors.

Interrupting Repetitive Behaviors

By training a dog to apply pressure on the child's arm for a brief section, you can help interrupt the behaviors. The Psychiatric Service Dog can be trained for specifically stopping these behaviors. They can use a voice command or a physical sign for a cue. Training the dog by action is pretty simple. Earlier, we discussed training a dog to retrieve items and then we discussed using anxiety cues to alert a dog to anxiety attacks. This is no different. In this situation, you can use a trigger such as the flapping and jumping of the child to trigger the dog to place a paw on the child. This works the same way it did prior.

*no copyright infringement intended

Clicker training method for interrupting behaviors in Autism patients

- Using the alert of jumping and flapping, connect it to the dog's nudge. If the dog nudges your hand, click the clicker and provide the dog with a treat.

- Using a verbal command that is associated with the jumping and flapping, allow the dog to respond to the command, and then nudge the hand. Next, click the clicker when the dog responds properly. Give the dog a treat.

- Manifest some jumping and flapping symptoms with the autistic child and use the verbal command cues to get the dog to respond with a nudge. Then, once the dog alerts with a nudge, click the clicker and provide a treat.

- Remove the verbal command and use the manifested jump and flap symptom so that the dog will identify the trigger. Next, continue to click the clicker in order to show the dog that there was a positive response, and then provide a treat.

- Remove the clicker from the alert command and use the cue for the jump and flap autism trigger to manifest the episode. When the dog responds properly, give the dog a reward for responding to the cue.

- Vary your practice in many various places, use distractions and various positions such as sitting, standing, and laying down. Continue to use step 3 if the dog is struggling with this process.

This can be modified to be used for many different triggers such as a repetitive word that is used by the patient or hitting their head repeatably. Either way, using the modification for behaviors in this technique will work amazingly. Since Psychiatric Service Dogs are trained very extensively, people often think that the dog is able to judge all situations. However, they are not able to be analytical and use reasoning. So, expecting them to protect your child from a dangerous situation is something that needs to be taught to them. Since the bond between a child and dog are strong, they will notice cues that will help keep the child pretty safe and redirect them in a positive way to another behavior.

Calming and Preventing Meltdowns

Another task that a Psychiatric Service Dog can do for an autistic child is helping them calm down or preventing a meltdown. They can be trained for aiding with meltdowns by applying pressure. In these situations, the dog can be asked to provide deep pressure by being trained to lay on top of the child in a comforting way. In the event that the child is crying, the dog would be able to recognize the sound and snuggle the child to help soothe and calm the child down. Oftentimes, the Psychiatric Service Dog will prevent or reduce the length of the meltdown. This can be done by applying the same steps as above except changing the trigger and response to a different one.

Below is a break down of how this will work. Remember when training your Psychiatric Service Dog that conditioning is the method with which you are able to train them. If they feel they are getting a positive result, they will be more than happy to help you with the services that you are teaching them. Dogs need positive reinforcement and thrive on a reward system. They will learn easier and be more willing to help you, especially since they are people pleasers.

Clicker Training method for detecting a crying child

- Identify that the child is crying and connect it to the nudge. If the dog nudges your hand, click the clicker and give the dog a treat.

- Using a verbal command that is associated with a crying child, teach the dog to respond to the command by nudging the hand and click the clicker when the dog responds properly. Give the dog a treat.

- Manifest some situation of the crying child and use the verbal cue along with the physical cue to get the dog to respond with a nudge. Then, once the dog alerts with a nudge, click the clicker and provide a treat.

- Remove the verbal command and manifest symptoms of the child crying. Once the dog nudges the child, continue to click the clicker and provide a treat. This shows the dog that there was a positive response.

- Remove the clicker and use the cue for the crying child to alert the dog to the child. When the dog responds properly, give the dog a reward for responding to the cue.

- Vary your practice in many various places. Use distractions and various positions such as sitting, standing, and lying down. Continue to use step 3 if the dog is struggling with this process.

- Once the dog has responded continuously with the same process, change the nudge to a deep pressure application and continue to train the dog for this service.

This task will fit the needs as defined by the Service Animal Law and would be allowed in a public building. This would provide extended amounts of service from the dog while the child is in overwhelming situations.

Training a dog to find you

Play hide and seek with your dog. This is the easiest way for your dog to learn how to find you. For instance, if you have an autistic child and you want the dog to be able to locate the child, train it to find the child. Children that are autistic tend to walk away often. You can quickly help your child to be found when they get lost if you have trained the dog to locate them

- To do this, hide the child behind a tree or wall and ask the dog to locate them.

- Do not allow them to make noises since the dog needs to learn to identify by their smell.

- Once the dog notices the child has disappeared, the dog will start looking for the child on their own. Some dogs may need more time than others to recognize that the child is gone, and others may first get anxious before looking for the child, especially if the child and the dog have bonded.

- This will trigger the dog's natural need to find the child.

- Once the dog starts looking for the child, you can have them make some small noises that will help the dog search. Since no one is completely quiet when they are out in the woods or lost in the home or neighborhood, it will help locate the child quicker.

- Once the dog finds the child, praise the dog for an excellent job and give it a treat.

- By using this method, you are training the dog that it is their job to locate the child when they wander away. Children tend to get lost often due to their natural curiosity. However, autistic children will wander away due to overstimulation or even just the fact that they are prone to bolting.

If you train them with a leash for this task, then the leash is helping with the training situation by speeding things up because your dog will notice that the child is gone by the reduced pressure on the leash.

Using a fenced in the backyard can provide a safer area to work in while keeping the dog in an area that is confined. This will also help with the child that is prone to wandering off. This is effective for both the child and the dog if they are not trained to stay with you. Training your dog how to pay close attention to you is part of the basic obedience training that you would have already provided your dog.

If your dog is having trouble finding the child in the beginning, then use a few sounds or noises to call their attention to the child and excite them in a way to encourage them to look for the child. Once they find the child, praise the dog for doing an excellent job. Making the lessons exciting and fun helps keep a slower dog more interested in learning faster and getting good at finding the child.

After playing this game of hide and seek a couple times a day, the dog should get the idea. At this time, you can then be quiet and give the dog a chance to realize you have not made any sounds to call the dog to you. This will entice them to start wandering around and looking for you. They will be interested in knowing what you are doing and where you are. Be sure to praise them with some treats or petting, and always say "good boy." Encourage them with play and allow them the time to learn to look for the child so they can develop a sense of connectivity to the child and finding it in times of need.

Playing at home is another way to do this task. Anytime the child wants to play with the dog, they can hide inside the house. This will make the dog look for the child. If the child makes noises, the dog will become alert and stand at attention. Then, they will go look for the child and when they find the child. The child can give them a treat. This makes it a game for both the child and the dog. Continue to praise the dog each time it locates the child. After a while, you can stop using noises to get the dog's attention and instead, wait for the dog to recognize and start looking.

You can also do this in another fun way by allowing the child to run away from the dog, and all of a sudden creating a concern for the dog. By calling the child as if the child is gone, the dog will start to look for the child. This will make them look for the child much quicker. Even though you make it seem like a game, they will feel a need to look. By making it a game, the dog is learning, and the child is not in danger. If you like, you can throw one of the dog toys for the dog to go after and then have the child hide while the dog is looking for the toy. The dog will go to collect the toy and come back looking for the child. This will prompt the dog to go look for the child.

You can also use a course for tracking to make the child disappear. AKC dogs tend to be tested on this for titles in tracking. This is often a learned skill that is taught to dogs that track their handlers first or it can be used as a practice in for learning how to follow an obstacle course.

You must make the trail or course yourself so that the dog smells your scent on the course. Then the child can travel the trail leaving a scent of them behind. This helps them make a map of the course for the dog to travel down looking for the child.

You can also use clothing to track the scent of an autistic child so that if it gets lost, the dog can find it. One way to do this is to let the dog see the kid wander off but use a shirt to give the dog the scent and let the dog track the child. This should be done with a freshly worn shirt and that is only touched by the child recently.

By leading the child on the obstacle course, you can drop pieces of clothing of that child so that the dog can track the child through smell. Walk slowly straight ahead in a line for 30 paces and then place another article of clothing that the dog will be able to sniff out and provide treats to reward your dog. Use the child's shoes to scruff the path as the child walks for 20 or 30 paces again, and then leave another scented item such as a toy or shirt. Make sure to give the dog treats as it continues to track.

By allowing your dog to learn to track your autistic child, you are also teaching the dog how to steer the child away from wandering off. Since autistic children tend to wander often, this can be a big deal to parents and can very overwhelming to the child as well when they find themselves lost in strange places.

Leading your dog from a starting point with clothes that smell like the child will help them to identify the child's whereabouts and gain the advantage for the next time they disappear. This is not only for children though. Several adults have severe autism that will cause them to walk off in the same manner. By making it a pattern to hunt the autistic individual, the dog will continuously look out for that individual and make sure that if they do not see them, they start to hunt them down to protect them.

Always encourage the Psychiatric Service Dog to continue forward with the search by allowing it to start the walk in the same direction where the next scented item is located. This allows you to simply tell your dog to find it, and they will head in the right direction from the beginning. It will go and find the trail of scented clothes easily and without trouble. Then, you should continue giving praise and treats, and this will encourage them to continue to look for the child. Over time, the dog will do it like it is second nature, and you can eliminate the reinforcements that are needed to get the dog excited about doing it.

After you have done this a few more times, you will be able to point the dog in the right direction without having to worry too much if the dog will find the child or not since the kid's clothing is scented and your dog will automatically follow the scent of the child or adult that is missing. Leaving a trail for every scented item of clothing helps to connect the dog's nose to the person they need to track and helps them locate places that you have been. This is exactly how the police train their dogs to locate prisoners that have run away.

Obsessive Compulsive Disorder behaviors cue with treats

- Nudge the dog's nose and reward the dog for the nudge.

- Command the dog to nudge and then add a reward for the dog's actions.

- Repeat this process until the dog has noticed the nudge.

- Change your position in order to train the dog for performing the alert in various locations and seated or standing positions. Reward the dog for each positive response.

• Decide on which Obsessive-Compulsive Disorder behaviors cue to use to help identify the Obsessive-Compulsive Disorder Behaviors. This can be scratching of your face or fidgeting, as well as rubbing your arms.

• Provide the anxiety cue and act as if the Obsessive-Compulsive Disorder Behavior symptom is real. Then, command the dog to nudge and reward for a positive response.

• Practice this over and over again the same way you would the retriever process. Then, start to recognize when your dog identifies the Obsessive-compulsive Disorder Behaviors cue without the command. Reward the identification instead of the command. Ignore any false alerts and shrug them off. Repeat this process several times per day for several weeks.

• As time progresses and the dog learns the trigger, remove the command altogether. Manifest an Obsessive-compulsive Disorder Behavior episode and leave out the command cue. Reward your dog when they respond appropriately.

• Practice in a variety of places and positions and continue to work with your dog until they are identifying regularly.

For PTSD

Training for Psychiatric Service Dog can be broken down into 13 effortless steps when applying deep pressure for a person that suffers from PTSD. PTSD is a debilitating disorder that prevents the sufferer from experiencing life and all that it has to offer. PTSD manifests in many different ways and can come from many different situations in life. Oftentimes, PTSD can come from the trauma that is experienced during war or experiences in life such as car accidents, sexual assault, abuse, and many other things.

PTSD patients have several unique needs that can be met by a Psychiatric Service Dog. These can include:

• Help block person in crowded areas

• Interrupting destructive behaviors

• Calm the handler using deep pressure therapy

• Provide security enhancement tasks (such as room search)

• Retrieve medications

• Deep pressure

These 13 effortless steps can mean the difference between living happily and suffering in fear every day while being stuck in your home.

Deep Pressure technique

•   Provide some delicious treats for your dog. Sit on the couch and begin to train your dog for the service that you need. By putting a treat in front of the dog's nose, you can slowly move the treat to the back of the couch. Once there, pat the couch back and repeat your dog's name with excitement.

•   Once the dog places their front paws on the couch, say "Up! Good!" and then reward the dog with its favorite treat.

•   If the dog is a medium-sized dog, you will need to have all four paws on the couch prior to repeating the command "up". Once they are on the couch, train them to lie down.

•   If the dog does not place there paws up at first, then you will need to work in stages and reward actions that bring the dog closer to the end result. For instance, when the dog places their head on the couch, place one paw on the couch, then eventually place all paw on the couch. Each time, keep on giving a treat to the dog until you get the result you need. This gets the dog to do a bit more each time. Eventually, the dog will have all the paws on the couch.

•   Continue to practice this action until the "up" command gets the result you are looking for. Then, continue until the dog does it without coaxing.

•   Once the dog is up, use the command "Okay, Good!" get the dog off the couch. Then proceed to praise the dog. If you use this every time the dog is told to get off the couch, they will learn it from repetition.

•   Next, lay down on the couch and use your hand and pat your lap or chest to call the dog up on you. Say "up!" At this time, the dog may be surprised or worried about climbing on you. It is a normal reaction. Give them a treat for anything that is a positive step towards the end result. Once they relax and understand, they will be less likely to stiffen up. You will have to lure them into this action since they will not be used to this.

•   A small to a medium dog can lie on the chest in a spoon or cuddling position with their head next to yours.

•   Once the dog has the hang of getting on top of your chest, practice the down command and get the dog accustomed to helping you with deep pressure.

•   Do not get frustrated with the dog. They are as new to this as you. If you find that you are frustrated, then stop and take a break. The key is to make this fun and not at all stressful.

- If you have to take a break, then start again later. Sometimes, the dog will get overwhelmed and needs time to recover. This training can take some time for them to adjust to.

- A large dog can apply deep pressure by putting his paws on either hip and lying across your lap or over your breast area.

- Each time your dog gets it right, extend the amount of time they lay there before giving the down command. Use treats and enforce the joy of the task. Eventually, you will be able to eliminate the treats and replace it with praises for a job well done.

If you are using a large dog, then you should teach them to push their head into your torso. Once they get used to the process, they will naturally cuddle you with their head moving closer to your torso. Praise them for this and give them a treat.

If the dog stands on his hind legs, then allow it time to rest its legs before you continue practicing. If you do have a full panic attack this time, rest may not be allowed but that is ok, the dog will get used to this eventually.

This technique can work with many different psychiatric conditions. Autistic, Depressed, Anxious, PTSD, and other patients can all benefit from this technique.

This book has given you several ways to train a dog for different services that will aid a disabled person with psychiatric needs. Dogs can be a terrific addition to your medical maintenance plan, and they can help give a person back their life. When someone is diagnosed with mental health issues, it can be even more devastating than having the illness. Imagine if you went from working full time to being confined to your home due to fear and panic attacks. Or what if you are moving along in life and then something traumatic happens and now you are suffering from PTSD.

How would you come to the realization that you may never work again or even get to experience the world like you are used to? This can be an excessively big blow to someone's ego and their social life. But with a Psychiatric Service Dog, you can start to take back the control that you have lost by this illness. Many people are suffering from some form of mental health and even more suffer from autoimmune disorders as well as medical problems such as diabetes. With the specialized training that can be provided to a dog for them to provide therapeutic service to the disabled, there is no limit to what people with illness can do now. You may not be able to work anymore, but at least you can try to experience a world without worry.

Post Traumatic Stress disorder cue with treats

- Nudge the dog's nose and reward the dog for the nudge.

- Command the dog to nudge and then add a reward for the dog's actions.

- Repeat this process until the dog has noticed the nudge.

- Change your position in order to train the dog for performing the alert in various locations and seated or standing positions. Reward the dog for each positive response.

- Decide on which anxiety cue to use to help identify the Post Traumatic Stress Disorder. This can be scratching of your face or fidgeting, as well as rubbing your arms.

- Provide the Post Traumatic Stress Disorder cue and act as if the Post Traumatic Stress Disorder symptom is real. Then command the dog to nudge and reward for a positive response.

- Practice this over and over again the same way you would the retriever process. Start to recognize when your dog identifies the Post Traumatic Stress Disorder cue without the command. Reward the identification instead of the command. Ignore any false alerts and shrug them off. Repeat this process several times per day for several weeks.

- As time progresses and the dog learns the trigger, remove the command altogether. Manifest a Post Traumatic Stress Disorder episode and leave out the command cue. Reward your dog when they respond appropriately.

- Practice in a variety of various places and positions and continue to work with your dog until they are identifying regularly.

Conclusion

Thank you for making it through to the end of *Training Your Own Psychiatric Service Dog*. I hope it was informative and provided you with all of the necessary tools you need to achieve your goals whatever they may be. Psychiatric Service dogs have been around for a while. And in the past 10 or so years, psychiatric patients have been training their dogs to provide the services as well. It used to be that you had to be blind or deaf to get a Psychiatric Service dog, but those days have passed. I hope this book provided you with the necessary information to help you train your dog and improve your life.

The next step is to start to figure out what exactly your Psychiatric Service Dog will be doing for you and start to look for the perfect Psychiatric Service Dog breed for your needs. Many people are not aware of the regulations that are associated with Psychiatric Service Dogs. Because of this, I have touched on that information within this book. I know that in order for you to be well prepared, you have to know what you are dealing with.

Few people know that they can train their own Psychiatric Service Dog and many people are getting ripped off. This book will hopefully put a stop to that. I hope that you learned how to figure out what the Psychiatric Service Dog breed you would like and also how to train the Psychiatric Service Dog at home for your specific needs.

Finally, if you found this book useful in any way, a review on Amazon is always appreciated!

Made in the USA
Coppell, TX
27 October 2020

40337099R00125